Searching in the Dark.

Some Light on the Subject.

A Wider View.

Keeping in Touch.

A Place in the Greenwood.

Pawprints across our History.-

**The original diaries are in the form of a collection of notebooks, charts, graphs and sketches and photographs compiled by Keith and Jane Childs.
During 1970 - 1984 watching was mainly in the Lower Wye Valley, Gloucestershire.
In the year 2004 watching was in the neighbouring Royal Forest of Dean, Gloucestershire.**

The Badger Diaries

Keith & Jane Childs

Keith Childs.
Nov. 2023.

The Badger Diaries

ISBN: 978-0-9556757-1-3

Published in the UK by
Bookworm Publications
www.bookwormpublications.co.uk

Printed in Great Britain by the
MPG Books Group, Bodmin and
King's Lynn

Dedication

To Jane and to Ben and Rosie

who have both inherited their mother's
warmth, charm
and intelligence. In their own ways they each
wrote this
book as much as I did.

Keith Childs.

SEARCHING IN THE DARK.

Full moon over the badger's wood.

By the Christmas of 1969 we had already spent several fruitless evenings trying to observe wild badgers before we actually saw our first one in the most tragic of circumstances. We had actually spent some hours on that very evening huddled silently in a copse at the head of a small valley that carries a bubbling brook into the River Wye.

In ignorance we were watching at the wrong time of the year to begin seeing badgers properly but the events of that evening were to deepen our resolve to see wild badgers in the Wye Valley, to become closely acquainted with them and to enrich our own affinity with nature by learning their ways and their lifestyle.

This book tells the story of our efforts to study the badgers of the brook, the triumphs and the achievements, the disappointments and the tragedies, and is our contribution to the understanding of this most endearing of animals.

As we drove home following the cold hours spent watching and waiting, I accelerated onto a straight stretch of road with open grassland on one side and woodland on the other.

There was a fleeting moment when I saw the low, grey figure racing head down across the headlights, and then a dull thud as the car struck our first wild badger a killer blow. Racing back up the road on foot we found her lying still and stretched full length in the gutter.

She was soft and warm with fresh mud on her paws and muzzle, her coat was wet with cool rain fresh from the grass of the pasture, but she was dead.

We could only lift her gently into the shelter at the foot of the hedge and go on home with our thoughts.

The next day we stopped briefly to examine her and she was still where we had lain her. We were glad and relieved that she had not recovered to crawl away in agony as many must do, but sad that she had lost the enchanting countenance carried the night before. We determined to devote time and energy to our study of the badger setts near the brook at every opportunity.

In the region of the brook there are several setts in good situations for watching but it seemed sensible to concentrate on one and hope that the badgers would get used to our smell and behave perfectly naturally with us present.

For some years we had walked regularly over the whole area of the valley and the sett that attracted us most was situated in the head of the valley where the brook itself is youthful and bubbling and the shady copse on the steep banks high above it makes a very pleasant place to spend an evening whether you see badgers or not.

We are highly qualified to make that statement having spent many evenings waiting for badgers from the Brook Sett.

Although we have been disappointed on the occasions when badgers have not been seen we have been thoroughly entertained by foxes, small birds, squirrels, owls, small rodents, insects visiting flowers and the whole panorama of the woodland community that perform for the patient observer.

The only time in our experience when badger watching, or rather waiting for badgers, becomes unpleasant is when darkness falls and nothing has been seen. Straining every sense to pick up signs of badgers in the dark is most demoralising; light and shade, faint noises, an object moving in the breeze can all have you believing there are badgers everywhere when there are none. Not being fully acquainted with the badger watcher's craft, we suffered much time wasted in this way and had to wait a long time before we finally saw badgers in September and then the diary simply reads...........

September 19th. 1970.
8.45 p.m. - Saw three at the Brook Sett all from entrances one and two.

We had not seen a great deal as it was dark and the badgers did not stay long at the sett. It was our only sighting of badgers in that first year of spasmodic watching.

Things did not improve until spring of the following year. In the meantime we decided to keep meticulous records of the setts and to conduct some experiments to establish some facts about times and conditions of badgers emerging from their setts and about their activities – "The Badger Diaries" were born. The methods and results of our investigations are explained here. It was a getting-to-know-you exercise!

Armed with a 3/6d. softback copy of Ernest Neal's monograph 'The Badger' we spent a great deal of our spare time trying to see badgers, but it slowly dawned on us that one man's experience is not another's guide to success.

It was apparent that there are no short cuts to acquaintance with wild creatures. Every scrap of evidence was vital if we were to develop an insight into the existence of the badgers at the brook.

Throughout 1970 and indeed, throughout the following years, we walked regularly over the Brook Sett and noted every detail of the changing scene. Which holes were used for digging? When were new holes opened? When were they enlarged or abandoned?

To keep a record of this information it was necessary to identify each hole and the identification procedure became a sometimes highly personalised business.

The holes with mounds of debris outside were called main holes and given a number e.g. M1, M2, etc. Smaller holes without a mound were called subsidiary holes and allocated a number similarly e.g. S1, S2, etc. However this method was soon supplemented by the naming of certain new holes.

We had a dog called Zabbie who loved the walks to the badgers as much as we did. In fact badgers became a substitute for walkies and produced the same excited clamouring that the more familiar term often does with dogs. Zabbie would always find new holes no matter how small or concealed, and one of his finds developed into a main hole which was to be the scene of much of our watching. Needless to say it is called Zabbie's hole.

When watching we used a ladder propped against one of the willow trees at the sett. In truth it was half a ladder that had been broken during fruit picking one autumn and which we commandeered as a watching seat. I stood at the bottom of the ladder using it as a rest and Jane sat at the top using me as a rest. It was highly effective and comfortable and served us for many years. One hole was dug on the far side of a holly bush behind this ladder and it was called the Ladder Hole.

Still other holes were called ventilation holes because they obviously provided no thoroughfare for the badgers but were invariably small holes venting out of the rooves of underground tunnels.

Perhaps a word is needed here on the definition of a sett. It is not at all clear what is meant when different observers talk about a sett but for our purposes it means a complex of holes, probably joined below ground by tunnels, and perhaps spreading over a large area.

The charts show the record of excavation at both the Brook Sett and at the smaller sett nearby called Aubrey's Sett.

They comprise an almost complete account of the badgers' work over a six year period from 1970 to 1975 inclusive.

At both setts the digging of new holes occurs clearly in two bands, from January to April and from July to November, although work at the smaller sett appears to be slightly behind that at the main Brook Sett.

The keeping of this information proved very valuable to the eventual success of our watching as it provided a clear picture of activity at the setts and guided us in deciding which holes to watch if we were to have the best chance of seeing badgers. We had a better idea of where they would very likely be.

We further used the information from the charts to construct maps of the Brook Sett to show how it has developed since the diaries were started in 1970. Following the progress like this helped us to adopt useful watching positions according to where the badgers were busiest.

The combined information from the charts and maps serves to illustrate how we were able to see badgers principally at the M1 hole during 1971, with activity increasing at M2 which was largely developed during that year. During 1972 the scene of most activity moved to Zabbie's hole, and the Ladder Hole behind our customary watching position was developed during 1973 and 1974.

M4 was also used a great deal for excavating debris. The most recent map, from 1982, shows the development of holes that have existed as ventilation holes since 1971. So by now we were getting to know where we needed to be and had some idea of what we were likely to see as the setts were worked on by a still fairly anonymous badger population.

A typical diary entry for this type of record keeping reads:

Notebook Mapping of the Brook Sett - 1970 ~ 1982 .

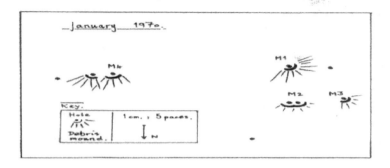

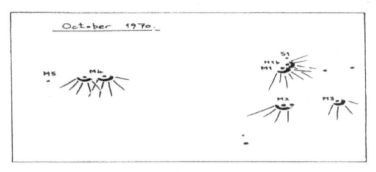

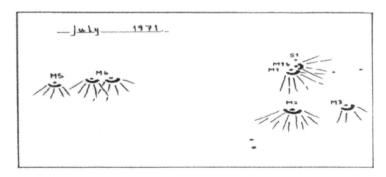

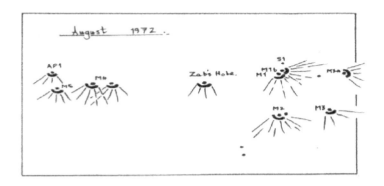

August 1972.

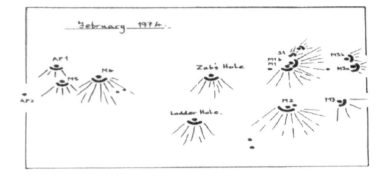

February 1974.

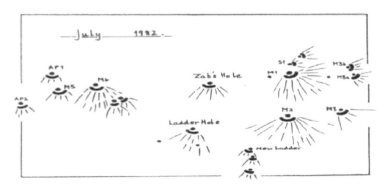

July 1982.

8

Sett Digging and Excavation – Aubreys Sett.

Listing all the holes from which digging took place in any month.

	1970	1971	1972	1973	1974	1975
January	Unknown	None	M.Os	Fa Fb	M4	None
February	M2	Spring Cleaning	None	M2 M1	None	Fa M2 V1
March	Unknown	None	Cleaning	M2 M4 Fa Fb	M2	Unknown
April	M1 M2	None	Sub1 Os filled in.	Fa Sub	M2 M4 New V hole	M2 Fa
May	M1 M2	M.Os	M2 M4	Fa	M2 Fa	M2 (fox)
June	None	Unknown	M2 M4 Os rabbits	Fa	None	M2
July	None	None	None	M2	None	Unknown
August	Fa Fb	M1 Fa	None	Fa M2	Unknown	M2
September	M2 M.Os	M2 Subs	None	Fa	Fa	None
October	None	Fa (fox)Two new V holes	Unknown	None	M4	None
November	None	M4	None	None	None	Unknown
December	None - Snow	None	Fb M4	None	None but occupied	Unknown

Red	Indicates a month in which new entrances were opened.

Sett Digging and Excavation – Brook Sett.

Listing all the holes from which digging took place in any month.

	1970	1971	1972	1973	1974	1975
January	Unknown	None	S1 M1v	None	M1b	Zabs
February	Cleaning M1b	M1	S1 M1 M4 M1v	M2	S1 S1b M3b M1b	Zabs AP1 M2 S4
March	Unknown	M1 M2 M3 M4	M1b M2 M4 M5	M1 Zabs M4 S4 AP1	S4 M3b M1b V1 V2	Unknown
April	M1 M2 M4 M5	M1 M2 M4 M5	S1 M1 M2 M4	M1 Zabs M4 S4 M2 AP1 S1	M3b S1 M2 V1 L	L Zabs
May	M1 M2 M4 M5	M1 M2 M4 M5 S4	M2 M1 S1	M4 S4 AP1 M1 Zabs M3	V2 AL1 AL2 M1 M3 L	L Zabs M2M3b M4 AP1
June	M1 M2 M4 M5	Unknown	M1 M2 M4 Zabs	M3 Zabs M4 S1	M2 M3 L	L Zabs M2 M3 V3
July	Unknown	M1 M2 M3 S4	M2 M1 M4 S4 AP2	M1 M2 M3 M4 L S1b	L	Unknown
August	M1 M2	M1 M2	M1b M2 M4	M1 M2 S1 L	Unknown	Unknown
September	M1 M2 New	M1 M2 M3 S4	S1 AP1	M1 M2 M3 L	M3 L	L M4 Zabs M3b
October	Two new become S1	M1 M2 Zabs	Unknown	L M2 M3 M4 V3 M3b	M3	M1b Zabs M4 L
November	None	M1 M3	None - Timber felling	None	None	Unknown
December	None - snow	M1 M3	S1	M1b	Zabs V3	Unknown

Red	Indicates a month in which new entrances were opened.

February 1974 Sunday 17th.

Violets, celandines and wood sorrel flowering.
Honeysuckle leaves just bursting from buds.
Daytime inspection.
Weather - very mild, no rain, bright sunshine following a damp spell. 9.6 inches of rain this year/4.4 inches usual.
Evening - dry, cold and very dark, no frost but giving way to frost early a.m.

**Aubrey's Sett in a field hedgerow
on a south facing slope.**

Brook Sett. Entrance M2.

**The mound outside Brook Sett M1
Entrance too high to see over.**

Brook Sett. Entrance M4.
Huge stones excavated.

Brook Sett
Much fresh soil and rocks from Sub. 1; ventilation hole above this used for soil and rocks and now enlarged. Far hole clear of leaves.

New main hole near M3 used for soil and rocks but not M3 itself.

Excavation from S1 has now nearly blocked off M1 except for a mere 4 inch ventilation hole. No excavation from M4, S4, hole above the path, Zab's. Ladder hole cleared but not used for excavation.

S1 and Zab's hole used for grass and foxglove bedding. Fresh dung pit at M3, much rooting in woods round about.

Aubrey's Sett

All area well flattened, paths in bracken field well padded and clear. No fresh digging or excavations.

Xmas 1970 and we had still only seen living wild badgers on one occasion, in September.

If we could have foreseen the events of the future ten years and the accusing finger of guilt pointing at Britain's badger population over the tuberculosis in cattle issue we would have had even more incentive to direct the limited time available toward badger study, but we were unaware of that cloud looming over the horizon and we continued to pursue our investigations alongside busy working and family lives.

In his book 'Watching Wildlife', David Stephen describes a method of establishing if a badger sett is used by laying sticks across the entrances and checking to see if they are moved. Over the Christmas period 1970 we employed his method at both the Brook and Aubrey's setts.

Early in the morning of each day we visited the setts and laid sticks across each entrance. On the following day we checked each entrance and noted where the sticks had been moved. The weather was also recorded and proved to be a reasonably hard spell for December.

The results of this investigation again show which entrances were being used and illustrate the activity of the badgers during a cold wintertime.

Aubrey's Sett is passed on the walk to the brook and is certainly a separate sett, being some 200 yards from the Brook Sett and on the other side of the valley. It is smaller and less frequently used than the Brook Sett and would appear to be an outlier to the main sett.

As the results show, it revealed no signs of occupation during the investigation of 1970 but was reinhabited on 13th. January 1971. This on/off occupation was a feature of our badger studies in the brook region.

The naming of Aubrey's Sett will be explained later but it figures intermittently throughout this account and affords a lot of understanding of our varied watching experiences.

The value of the results of the Xmas 1970 experiment impressed us deeply, so much so that at Xmas 1974 we repeated the experiment. The results are included here and show an increase in activity compared with 1970 which we attributed directly to the milder conditions. They serve also to illustrate the growth in size of the Brook Sett (number of holes) and they show positive signs of occupation at Aubrey's Sett.

In Xmas 1970 the badgers at the Brook Sett stayed down for three nights out of eight. It was a hard winter and a cold spell. The main hole M1 was used on each night that badgers came out.

At Aubrey's the sticks were not moved enough to allow emergence at any of the holes, but were disturbed at two holes on separate nights. We thought it was not occupied, especially as this is a south facing slope which thaws more readily in hard weather - an observation that was to prove relevant to badger movements.

STICKS EXPERIMENT AUBREY'S SETT 1970.

Thursday 24th. _ Thursday 31st. December.

Hole / Date	M1	M2	M3	M4	O.S.	S1	S2	S3	S4	S5
24										
25										
26										
27										
28										
29										
30									D	
31										D

*	Sticks knocked down – Nil.	D	Sticks disturbed.

STICKS EXPERIMENT AUBREY'S SETT 1974.

Tuesday 24th.- Tuesday 31st. December.

Hole / Date	M1	M2	M4	Fa	Fb	V1	O.S.	V2	V3
24		*	*		*	*			
25		*	*	*		*			
26		*	*	*		*			
27		*	*	D			D		
28		*	*	*		*			
29			D	*					
30		*		*					
31									

*	Sticks knocked down.	D	Sticks disturbed.

16

STICKS EXPERIMENT BROOK SETT 1970.

Thursday 24th. – Thursday 31st. December.

Hole	M	M	M	M	M	S	S	S	S	S	
Date	1	2	3	4	5	1	2	3	4	5	Overnight Weather
24											Light snow 10 pm. Very cold .
25	*	*							*		Snow am. Variable temperature.
26											Heavy snow am. Very cold – 6c.
27											Mild 10 pm. Freezing am.
28	*	*		D	*				*		Thaw ~ fields clear. Drizzle/cold wind.
29	D										Snow 7~10 pm. Mild.
30	*			*					*		Very hard frost before 9 pm. Clear
31	*										Frosty & clear.

*	Sticks knocked down.	D	Sticks disturbed.

STICKS EXPERIMENT BROOK SETT 1974.

Tuesday 24th. _ Tuesday 31st. December.

Hole Date	M 1a	M 1b	M 1v	M 2	M 3	M 3b	S 1	S 1b	V	Z	M 4	S 4	A P 1	A P 2	V 1	V 2	V 3	L	Weather
24		*		*	*					*	*	*	*		*			*	Clear breezy cool
25		*		*						*	*	D	*		D		D	*	Clear Windy pm. Rain am.
26		*		*	*	*	*	*		*	*	*	*					*	Heavy rain High wind
27				*			*	D		*	D	*	D					*	Windy Damp
28		*		*			*	*		*	*	*	D	D				*	Windy Rain
29		*		*	*	*	*	D		*	*	*	*	*	D		*	*	Windy Drizzle
30		*								*	*	*	*		D			*	Clear Still Frost am.
31		*		*			*	*		*	*	*	*				D	*	Still No frost

*	Sticks knocked down	D	Sticks disturbed

In the milder Xmas of 1974 the records show that at the Brook, two holes were used each night and a further four holes were used on seven nights out of eight. One hole was used on six out of eight nights. Besides these notable results, use of the sett was general with only four holes not used at all, three of those being small ventilation holes not used as thoroughfares.

At Aubrey's in 1974 only one hole was not used at all, but on 31st. December the badgers were either not there or they stayed down, for no sticks were disturbed - perhaps they had gone to a party! During the week all the other five holes were used.

By the New Year 1971 things were beginning to take shape. We had positive records of the badger's activities and a clear picture of where to watch in 1971. When to watch was a problem that still needed solving.

The walk to the Brook Sett is about a mile and takes us across fields to a narrow winding metalled lane that climbs steeply to the head of the valley. Standing on a south facing slope of the valley, to the left of the lane is a sun drenched, whitewashed farm cottage which may easily have been taken straight from the pages of a children's storybook. Just inside the iron gate that closes the cottage path from the lane is a well with an iron lid on huge hinges that swing open like double doors. The concrete path is lined on both sides by brightly coloured flowers and amongst the flowers on the left hand side are several white beehives. The resident bees produce the most delicious honey, a small jar of which our children occasionally received as a gift when we visited the cottage. Adjoining the path and hives is an orchard containing traditional chicken houses on wheels.

The whole cottage scene smacks of days gone by. As you step inside the cottage you enter a room dominated by a splendid grandfather clock, a room extremely homely and pleasing for its sheer simplicity.

Whenever we visited, the gentleman of the house always sat in his accustomed place beside the black open range at one end of the room.

His name was Aubrey Keedwell and we became acquainted through a mutual love of badgers. He regaled us with stories of old badgers of the district as we sat absorbed in the timeless atmosphere of his home. He also told us of a sett under his barn that used to be inhabited by three old badgers that would pass him in single file grunting as they went.

This was, apparently, a regular occurrence as he made his way home from the local inn with his faithful dog Judy. Further stories told us of a mystified local farmer surveying 1/4 acre of churned up meadow and how he had reassured the farmer that,

"It is Mr. Badger in there after the cockchafer grubs you see. He's a doing good work here."

He also told us how he once set a snare to catch a fox that was taking his chickens. By mistake he caught a badger and it upset him for weeks afterwards. We felt a great affinity with Aubrey, as we shared his grief at the needless death of a badger. The field we had to cross to reach the Brook Sett belonged to Aubrey and the small outlier sett of which we have spoken is situated in the hedgerow of that field. Once he was sure that we meant no harm to the badgers, he readily gave us permission to walk all of his land and so we called the sett in the hedgerow Aubrey's Sett.

As springtime arrived our watching became more profitable as we saw badgers several times during March and April, but they were mostly brief glimpses and afforded little information about the colony living at the Brook Sett. Our notes of the occasions are all much alike and 14th. April is a good example:

Hot day, still evening, dull moonlight. Watching at the Brook Sett Entrances M1 and M2. Two badgers from direction of entrances M4 and M5 at 7.50 GMT. Dispersed into woods around new latrine. Much underground noise of scuffling, grunting and bumping at M1. Faces seen at entrances M2 and M3 for brief spells. Did not emerge fully again before we left at 8.30 GMT. Crashing all around - badgers from M4/M5 region.

March had seen the beginning of much work by the badgers at the Brook with them excavating huge piles of sandy red soil mixed with great boulders as big as three fists and preparing matted scoops of bedding material which they left going in or straggling out of sett entrances. The record of badgers actually seen remained much as we have described, with unsatisfactory sightings in poor conditions. We were becoming impatient as May came in! Then the events of the year unfolded further.

We vividly remember the 8th May for we had negotiated all the barbed wire fencing and were picking our way up the bank above the stream at 7.30 GMT, as always seeking out the mossy patches and bared tree roots to tread on, making our approach as soundless as possible.

Cubs playing at the sett entrance Brook Sett May 1971

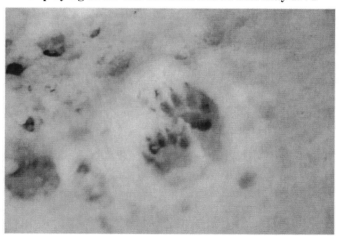

Tracks in the snow

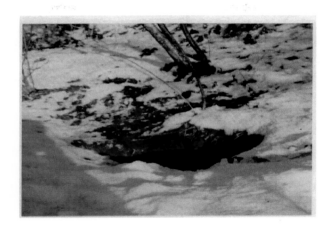

Brook Sett. Entrance M1. Xmas 1970.

Rosie Childs
A muddy pathway - especially one with a drying top
surface can hold clues to badger activity.

We were equipped for a long wait following over two hours of fruitless watching on the previous night. Still we made the usual wary inspection of the sett area.

Clearly silhouetted against the background greenery was a cub badger. He was rigidly still; facing away from the sett and two others were squabbling in the well where the ground slopes steeply into the entrance.

For no apparent reason the cub suddenly leapt off all four feet and turned to join the affray that was the other two. Then he was out of it, attacking the willow saplings and sniffing at the ivy growing there.

The two in the entrance well were standing head on and daring each other with both front feet rigid and scuffing the soil as they wriggled backwards grunting almost fiercely, while the third chased his tail at insane speed only feet away.

At intervals in their play it seemed that their legs could hold them no longer and they wobbled helplessly back into the entrance, in and out of which they bounded rehearsing scenes of alarm.

After twenty-five minutes the first cub disappeared below ground not to be seen again that evening, closely followed by the others. Although we waited until 10 o'clock we saw or heard nothing more and left wondering how to account for the evening's events.

Had the whole family been out in the afternoon sun which the diary recalls was *very hot with no wind* and the cubs been last to retire? Had the adults left the cubs and gone away into the woods to forage? Were the parents underground and reluctant to emerge on such a pleasant evening?

We were spurred on to make a watch on the afternoon of the ninth, but saw nothing and the only other occasion that year on which we saw similar behaviour was well on into September, the eleventh to be exact:

Weather - Day - warm and dry as for previous week, Evening - cool but still. Arrived at the Brook Sett at 7.20 to find three cubs out at entrance M1. Rough play and yickering around the play tree.

Cubs saw us approach through briars - were inquisitive but not alarmed – came to approximately three feet to sniff. Not alarmed by distant gunshots. No sign of adults. Watch abandoned at 8.20 due to proximity of gunshots.

Tiny cub prints possibly too light for the claws to make an impression. Rosie Childs.

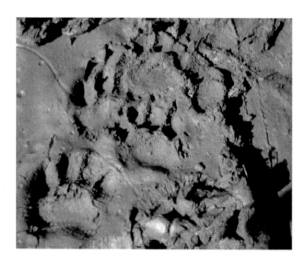

**Adult paw prints complete with claw marks
forward of the pad marks.
Rosie Childs**

As this is off the beaten track and rarely disturbed, we are inclined to favour the possibility of the badgers having been out in the afternoon sun and that we saw the end of their day.

Surely the adults would not have left their cubs for so long, especially on the May occasion when they were so young. The diligence of the adults in caring for their young is usually very apparent in these early days and a sequence of events witnessed quite frequently demonstrates this nicely.

It was late May in 1971 and still daylight when the boar emerged at 8.00 pm. and departed for the woods and latrine above the sett. At 8.45 he returned to the sett entrance to make a distinct purring sound.

Immediately the sow and one cub emerged, boldly and without caution, and two other cubs joined them from a nearby subsidiary entrance to make the family group complete. It was as if they were waiting for the boar to return and sound the all clear.

There was a period of robust play amongst the cubs while the boar and sow treated themselves to a playful mating attempt, and by 9 o'clock the parents had got the youngsters into orderly file by purring and by the boar physically knocking them into line with his snout. The ragged family column, led by the sow with the boar at the rear, retraced his earlier steps into the woods.

The guttural purring must be a request or command note as the cubs always respond to it by going to or following a purring adult.

This family of five were living at the Brook Sett in May 1971 and then, as if by magic, there were eight badgers; the family of five and three others.

Although this was not immediately clear we soon saw the two groups separately - two adults with three cubs and two adults with one cub.

Something that suggested that the family of three were newcomers was their extreme caution compared with the others who were becoming accustomed to us.

The female was very cautious, often emerging late and, after warily joining the community activities, retiring below ground when the others left for the surrounding woods and fields. Also the cub was much smaller and more bad tempered. He was easily recognisable and made our observations easier to interpret than they would have been without him as a landmark.

The fact that setts often accommodate large numbers of badgers living as a community group during the July/August time of year is known as the period of community living. It is far more marked in some instances than others and its significance is not altogether clear, although pairing of badgers and the digging of new setts seems to coincide with this period.

Perhaps it is to facilitate pairing or to allow familiarisation between members of the community and the strengthening of the bonds that exist between individuals or groups within the community. After all the badger is a strongly territorial animal and must be familiar with the creatures it is going to tolerate.

It has also been suggested that this period is set aside for the scouring and airing of other quarters before the winter months.

July now, and watching becomes a good excuse for sitting in the woodland soaking up the evening sunlight. Arriving at about 6.30 the air is heavy with the stench of stinkhorn fungi, especially pungent if the vegetation is damp. The mellow sunlight winks and flashes through the full leaf canopy of silver birch and elm wavering in the silent breeze, felt only by them at their majestic height above us - the breeze is working a solar light show in this shady place.

It is absorbing to stand silently and watch the bees methodically working the tall, erect stems of foxgloves, visiting each open flower to steal away its nectar and unwittingly perform the essential duty of pollination. The visit of a small bird might distract us for a while - perhaps a willow warbler circling the low vegetation of briar, foxglove and fern searching for insects.

It utters its *hew-ett, hew-ett* call and would momentarily fascinate us with its trick of alighting on a fern frond and riding up and down as the stem recoils under the tiny weight.

The first calls of the tawny owls are a feature to note, as is the arrival of the grey squirrel in its drey high in the branches of the ivy clad silver birch.

The chance passing of a fox or the chattering of woodmice on a nearby tree stump adds richly to the scene.

Thus time passes quickly to the moment of the first indications that the badgers are ready to emerge - usually a bumping or scuffling underground and yelping if cubs are there.

Such was the scene that awaited us in July 1971 with the badgers well and truly cemented into a community and the small cub enjoying the company of the others.

On the 30th. it was 7.30 and still broad daylight when two cubs emerged from the main sett. They proceeded to clean and scratch and, of course, play now quite roughly with much pained yelping. Four minutes later and the boar emerged to assert his authority with a purring and clicking that halted the cubs while he surveyed the scene. Soon there were six, being two adults and four cubs who left in ragged file for the undergrowth.

Five more minutes and another adult followed them only to return, collect his mate and hurry after them again. By 8.15 it was an empty stage and we left for home.

The last adult was the cautious female, the one who padded nervously in and out of the sett after the others had dispersed for the evening.

So it became a feature of our watching to wait on after the others had gone because we knew there was another badger to see.

She even appeared huddled and withdrawn in her nervous attitude except on the few occasions when she would join the others and the whole community of eight would forage together.

Our records show that the cubs were regularly out before their parents by this time. Almost every watch in July saw the cubs out first but always to be joined by adults in a few minutes providing fair indication of the independence they had achieved. The cubs were restless, full of energy, inquisitive and always seeking to emulate their parent's behaviour. They possessed all the qualities that make young animals so endearing, the subjects of great love and affection.

The months of high summer were best for observing badgers going about their everyday chores with cubs virtually free to roam unsupervised by late August.
But by 27th the colony showed little of the unity in their behaviour witnessed in July.......

Friday 27th. Weather - Day - quite warm as for two days previously. Evening - warm but breezy. Arrived at Brook Sett at 8.10. It is dusky. Immediately noises underground near M1 and M2.

8.20 Two from M1 trotted off in direction of M4/M5. May have startled into there after scenting us.

8.25 The small cub followed them in much less cautious manner - stopping to sniff and forage.

8.40 The big boar emerged from M1 and the small cub returned. Boar left casually for woods above the sett followed by his mate and a third badger in a short while.

9.00 Heard noises near area of flattened grass noticed above the sett. Two badgers were working there and in poor light conditions we listened to them collecting and carrying nine bundles of bedding back to M1. Shadowy figures, hunched, labouring over loads of green vegetation, shuffling backwards to carry it home. This was a scene of intense industry that we left behind us for our homeward Journey.

Aubrey's sett reoccupied on August 2 (badger tracks), then by foxes on October 2nd (fox tracks).

The unfortunate lack of a record for June leaves an uncertainty over the exact onset of *community life* but they are together during July. The big boar, the small cub, and the group of three cubs have been easy to identify. Sadly we had to admit that the only two badgers we could identify now, in the poor light of late evening, were the big boar and the very small cub and the colony was moving separately, in pairs and threes and they did not tarry long at the sett before moving off to other activities and locations.

Although we made visits in September and August to witness industrious scenes similar to those of late August, watching was becoming less and less rewarding and we returned to keeping the record books of evidence collected during daytime visits and we waited eagerly for the next springtime evening when we could further our determined association with wild badgers.

It had been very much a matter of trial and error whether we saw badgers during the early months of our watching. We worked on the assumption that the badger was an almost exclusively nocturnal animal only emerging from its sett well after sunset and returning at dawn, so offering the watcher little opportunity to observe it at length.

31

Combined with the fact that we first attempted to see badgers in the winter months when that assumption could largely be found to be true we had realistically reduced our chance of success to a very low chance indeed.

As described it was only when we determined to arrive early at the sett, much earlier than we deemed absolutely necessary, that we stumbled on badgers already out playing in the evening sunlight and realised that we may have frightened badgers in rather than frightened them from coming out on many spring and summer evenings.

Badgers at the Brook Sett ~ 1971 . Changes in Numbers and Evidence for A Period of Community Life.

FROM M1 or M2	FROM OTHER ENTRANCES	DATE
2 adults	2 adults	March 27
2 adults		April 11
2 adults		April 12
1 adult and cub noises		May 1
3 cubs		May 8
2 adults, 3 cubs		May 30
4 adults, 4 cubs		July 3
2 adults, 3 cubs	2 adults, 1 cub	July 10
4 adults, 4 cubs	*This period*	July 17
4 adults, 4 cubs	*indicates the*	July 3
2 adults and cub noises	*peak period for the colony*	August 2
3 adults, 3 cubs	*living together*	August 4
6 to include the small cub and the big boar	*as a single community*	August 27
3 cubs		September 11
2 cubs		October 2

Once we had discovered the probable time of emergence from the sett we were able to arrive in good time and be settled in our watching places well before faint underground noises heralded the first badger of the evening.

As we became more adept at estimating emergence times we were able to reduce the amount of time between arriving and the emergence of the first badger to about twenty minutes. To facilitate more accurate estimation of emergence times from year to year we began to keep careful records for future reference. Every time we saw the first emergence of the evening we noted the time and entered it on a master chart which was pinned to the wall at home. All the times were converted to GMT, for ease of interpretation to any given year.

Our chart, reproduced here, shows the time at which the first badger of the evening was seen to definitely leave its sett, except on those occasions when the badgers were already out when we arrived at the sett. Those times are marked with an asterisk and are included to give guidance on the time when the watcher should arrive at the sett.

We have been able to use this chart successfully to estimate the time at which we should arrive at the sett in any period of the year for which we have previous records of watching badgers.

We still find watching in the winter months unprofitable due to irregular and unreliable emergence times and the fleeting glimpses of badgers that even great patience affords, and hence we have no records of times from November to February.

When the times are presented as a scatter graph it can be seen that the badgers at the Brook emerge from their setts at quite regular times throughout the period from late March to late August. The times become notably earlier in the months of September and October until our records run out at the end of October.

Notebook Scatter Graph

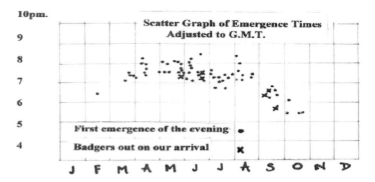

Our graph compares very favourably with E. G. Neal's graph in The Badger monograph and he points out the close relationship of emergence times to sunset times, the sunset occurring approximately between thirty and ninety minutes before emergence although, as we have seen, it is not always that straightforward.

Equipped with an accumulating picture of life at the Brook Sett we were pleased to discover that we could use whatever spare time we had to visit the badgers with a reasonable certainty of seeing them.

Thus we were able to accommodate such events as moving house, changing jobs, the birth of our children and other all consuming activities without losing track of the badger colony. Reference to our diary of the setts would soon put us back on the trail after long spells of absence.

In this way we have maintained a periodical observation of the badgers at the brook and the notes we made allow us now to offer first hand observations of many of the routine activities carried out by them.

Times When Badgers Were First Seen Emerging G.M.T.

February	27	6.25
March	18	7.05
	27	7.45
	28	7.30
	31	7.25
April	2	7.17
	10	8.15
	11	8.00
	12	7.40
	14	7.50 8.00
	15	7.20
May	1	7.40
	4	8.05
	8	7.40 *
	11	8.00
	12	7.30
	23	8.10
	26	8.07
	28	7.40
	29	8.00
	30	7.50 7.45 7.25 7.45
	31	7.55 7.25* 7.40

Continued from page 35

June	4	7.15
	7	7.35
	8	8.02
	10	8.15 7.50 7.55
	12	7.05
	19	7.04
	21	7.30
	22	7.30*
	23	7.15* 8.30
	24	7.10
July	2	7.30
	3	7.45
	8	7.20
	10	6.50
	13	7.20
	14	7.05
	17	7.10
	19	7.25
	21	6.47
	27	7.20
	30	7.30
August	2	8.30 7.07
	4	7.40
	6	8.00
	8	7.10
	10	7.25
	27	7.20 7.20
	28	7.30

Continued from page 36

September	9	6.25*
	11	6.40*
	14	6.17
	16	6.55
	19	6.45
	20	5.55*
	23	6.30
October	2	5.30
	6	6.05
	23	5.30
	26	5.35

Emerging at Dusk: Brook Sett

SOME LIGHT ON THE SUBJECT.

Sunset over the valley and the brook.

Noises and
Communication

During our watching we have been particularly fascinated by the range of sounds badgers make. We have been able to relate several particular sounds to a definite response amongst a group of badgers playing or foraging together and the responses are often more pronounced when adults are supervising cubs.

On numerous occasions a low purring sound made by an adult at the sett entrance has brought out other badgers from the sett. Throughout March and April this sound was used to call out other badgers and during July it was used by the boar to call out the sow and cubs.

This often happened when the boar had left the sett first to visit the latrines in the woodland and then returned to collect his family. On July 10th. and 30th. 1971 we heard the same sound used to control the cubs and call them into line and order, and on one occasion in July the sow joined her mate at work near the sett entrance and then visited a separate entrance to call out the cubs.

A quite different sound is used as a warning when danger is suspected. On April 11th. we were detected while the boar was at the sett entrance and he produced a definite tic, tic, tic to warn the others from coming out. This sound is rather like the noise made when your teeth are clinking together or chattering with cold.

On other occasions a combination of the two sounds, rather like purring with your teeth chattering, was used to halt the cubs play completely while the adult listened and sniffed the air. As soon as the adult relaxed so did the cubs and activity resumed.

The cubs seem to have a limited range of sounds. While playing and wrestling a very noticeable yic, yic, yicker is made interspersed with pained yelps when one is hurt more than usual. This yickering can often be heard long after a family has dispersed into the woods and fields and is a characteristic sound at a badger sett in summer.

On *10th. July 1971* we startled a cub by moving carelessly when he approached from a short distance......................

Weather - hot, dry and still as it has been all week. 7.35 - arrived at Brook Sett and set up camera on the play tree.

7.50 - broad daylight - one restless cub emerged alone from M1. walked towards pylon area.

8.05 - Cub returned at a steady trot - seemed to be chasing midges - returned to M1.

8.06 - still broad daylight - boar, sow and three cubs left immediately for pylon area. Cubs playing roughly all around our feet.

8.10 - I moved to watch them go and startled a cub who detected me. He crouched on his hind legs, hissed, growled.

Then wriggled backwards while moving his head from side to side before turning and tearing headlong into the sett.

As the cubs grew this growling, hissing and threatening posture became more prominent in rough play. Baring of the teeth also became prominent.

An interesting aside is the fact that no scent was noticed on this occasion as it is so often when the cubs are engaged in rough play or badgers are generally alarmed.

The cub I startled was small and had joined the community with his parents late in the year. We wonder if emission of scent is a sign of maturity?

When adults romp, growling, snorting and snapping are more pronounced than yickering which is rarely heard from adults. Noises from underground were very commonly heard while waiting for badgers and hollow thumps, yelps and scuffles often announced the arrival of the first badger. We have also noticed that an alarmed badger racing into its sett thumps the ground with its feet to make a hollow warning signal.

By contrast the animals darting in and out during play rarely make this noise indicating that it is not the speed alone which causes the stamping.

We think this could act as an effective warning system. Our observations on the sounds made by badgers show that they can communicate moods, discipline, fear and contentment among themselves, in fact they make a very good job of conveying emotional feelings. We understood the messages and so did the badgers in the community we have watched.

A fragile fungus in the sett entrance – not used recently.

Who Goes There ~ Friend or Foe?
Scenting and Musking.

Phil Drabble writes that badgers (wild) never wander far on strange land without squatting as if in deep meditation. This is really to *spot* a minute drop of musk every few yards to mark the territory they cover. When they want to return all that is necessary is to hunt their own line of spots back to the point of departure.

Paget and Middleton say that objects such as stones, sticks or the ground itself are musked, helping the badgers find their way around and acting as a method of territorial marking. Neal explains how the work of Frank on musking shows that repeated musking when travelling from a sett builds up a series of scent trails which act as highways to the badgers living there. They lead to places of particular importance such as feeding grounds. On reaching its destination the badger then leaves the scent trail and forages more widely. Later it searches around until it picks up the home path once more.

Paget and Middleton also reported that one badger repeatedly laid musk on a path where the observer had inadvertently trod an hour earlier.

George Barker's experiment with substituting dung from one social group with that from another showed how the resident badgers became very upset and urinated and defecated on top of the foreign dung.

The Ministry of Agriculture research programme in Gloucestershire has shown that badgers mark their territory by depositing dung in latrine pits at its boundaries and Drabble further explains how a wild boar attempted to lay down territory right up to fences which formed the extent of his badger's compound by making dung pits adjacent to the fence.

It is therefore accepted that badgers mark their territory with spots of musk deposited from glands situated near the tail and by the systematic depositing of dung. They also lay trails which enable them to find their way around and they use musk scent to reinforce their claim to territory and to warn off intruders.

Scent marking also takes place between members of a social group and serves as a process of identification between members of that particular group.

Our observations both support these accepted theories and provide new examples to add to the understanding already achieved.

Throughout our diary notes we have frequently added as an adjunct to the main activities described that there was a strong musky smell on the air following play or communal grooming sessions. Sometimes we have been able to hear and smell badgers but have not been able to see them. It seems that adults and cubs involuntarily emit scent when excited in vigorous play or grooming, but that they can voluntarily discharge scent when marking territory, routes or other members of their social group. Many observers have reported incidents of scenting but the sequence of events we should like to report is important because it tells of a time when musk smell and communal scenting routines became particularly evident, and for very sound reason.

May 30th. 1975

Weather - Day - fine, hot, wind free, Evening - cool, still, frost later. Arrived at Brook Sett at 7.25 GMT. Watching at the holly bush.

7.27 - One badger from the Ladder hole, followed by four others - all adults. Great scratching session - communal grooming in pairs and threes.

7.45 Two left for Zabbie's hole - much moving between Ladder hole, Zab's. M4 etc. - some bedding taken in at Zab's. and AP1. Every time badgers met during this period of movement they performed a scenting routine which left a strong smell of musk on the air.

8.15 All had left except for two adults who stayed at the Ladder hole. Six adults seen but no cubs. Time spent at sett - approx. 50 mins.

The badgers lay scent on each other by raising their tails and rubbing their hind quarters against one another. Sometimes the hind leg of one is cocked over the other for scenting. As described, the community at the Brook Sett scented each other meticulously on May 30th. until every badger had been actively involved.

On June 1st. we made a daytime inspection and as we climbed the stile to the brook a strong musky smell filled the air.

All around the sett area the ground was heavily scented and on the mound outside entrance M1 we found a small patch of flattened grass which was heavily stained with blood and matted with badger hair and some other redder tufts of fur which we thought were fox.

The air was rather unpleasant to breathe so heavy was the smell of musk scent and so we made a quick count of holes in use and started to leave suspecting that the cause of the meticulous scenting of individuals and territory had been a fight at M1.

As we climbed down the bank between the sett and the brook we found a dead badger. The body was somewhat decayed but the entrails were still present. At a later date we collected the skull and estimated that it was a two/three year old male.

Two thoughts occurred to us - an alien badger had visited the sett to be attacked and driven off to where it had died - the scenting of May 30th. would have been justified as a means to identification of acceptable individuals within the community. Or, the two distinct types of fur at the bloodstained scene suggested a skirmish with a fox which the fox had won. To add credence to this theory Aubrey Keedwell told me that evening that a vixen had brought cubs to the badger's sett in his field.

He was referring to Aubrey's Sett - the small outlier to the Brook Sett.

Had the vixen been the subject of aggression from the badgers and, having killed or mortally wounded the badger, decided to take her cubs away from the danger area?

The mystery remains unsolved but we are inclined to favour the theory of a conflict between badgers and foxes largely because of events which subsequently came to light concerning badgers and foxes at the Brook Sett.

We had often read that fox and badger paths frequently cross in the wild and that they would even inhabit the same sett although they tended to go their separate ways rather than share activities.

Early in our watching we saw foxes using the same paths, sometimes crossing the sett whilst we waited for badgers to emerge.

The first time we saw a fox at the Brook Sett was in July 1970 when it was still light at approximately 8.00 GMT. We did not hear a sound or see any movement of vegetation as the fox travelled the badger path.

Badger remains found near the Brook Sett June 1975.

All we could see was the red/brown colour of his back as he glided stealthily along. We thought it was one of the corgis who were family pets and were cursing that we would have to abandon the watch to take the dog home when the whole creature came into view - a young fox who drifted silently away.

Since then we have observed several similar close encounters in August, April, May and June with the August incident providing a particularly close call as the badgers emerged only two minutes after a fox had crossed the sett. They showed no interest in the fox trail but were very interested in the path we had walked that day with our two dogs.

We rarely attempt to watch on the night following a daytime visit and the evening was duly spoilt by the obvious disquiet of this first badger - he detected our earlier presence and retreated below ground. That was all we saw that night.

The association between the resident foxes and badgers became more intense in 1977 when the presence of foxes in the brook region became a feature of our watching and provided a great deal of interest.

The first episode in this Year of the Foxes took place on April 24th. when we had arrived early determined to stay as late as necessary. At 7.25 GMT. an adult fox arrived and began to pick its way down across the sett towards the brook. The instant it came to the path that we had used to walk to reach the sett it stopped, sniffed and ran silently into the Ladder hole. We did not see it come out but it may have gone unnoticed through another exit. We assumed it was a fortunate sighting of a fox taking refuge in a badger sett as is often reported. It fell dark and seeing or hearing nothing we left, puzzling a second consecutive blank watch.

On May 4th. we had waited for an hour before two adult badgers emerged from Zabbie's hole at 8.05. There was remarkably little activity and they departed in a subdued manner. Something was definitely amiss and was affecting the badger's behaviour but we did not yet suspect association with foxes.

It was not until a daytime inspection at 2.00 o'clock on May 8th. that we saw two fox cubs playing in the valley of the seasonal brook that is a tributary to the main brook. We stopped short of the sett and watched them for a long while during which time they came very close to us before one romped off up the valley and the other disappeared into the Brook Sett.

Close inspection of the sett showed that M2, M3, Ladder hole and S1 were all occupied by foxes or rather by their distinctive smell! It was then that we realised that our badgers were entertaining foxes in their sett and our appetites were whetted in the hope that we might see some of the action reported from other jointly occupied setts. Perhaps we should enjoy some exciting evenings like that witnessed by Monica Edwards when she saw a boar badger bring a limp vixen out of the sett in its mouth and then return underground with it, later to bring his replete family above ground to laze near the sett as if they had overeaten.

Our next visit was delayed until May 23rd. when we were delighted to see three adult badgers emerge from Zabbie's hole at 8.10 and begin to scratch and groom in the dappled evening sunlight. Suddenly they were alert, one of them staring intently down at M2 which was out of sight, and he ran down there. Silence!

The other two retired below ground and we waited expectantly.

Nothing! Decided to move around to watch at S1 which we had done successfully before when badgers had been active but out of sight in that direction. Once again the two fox cubs were out playing and we watched them wondering what was their relationship with the badgers.

We did not see badgers again that night but we kept the fox cubs company until darkness fell.

By June we had still not seen any cubs with the adult badgers and we began to resolve that there were none that year. We continued to enjoy the foxes although by June 23rd. there was no smell of foxes occupying the Brook Sett. On August 2nd. we were creeping along the brook at 6.50 when we spotted the two fox cubs leaping about in the brook and stalking each other, sniffing everywhere, balancing and wrestling.

They were quite well grown now with a proper brush developing. One had a dark brush and the other was fair. We watched them for a few minutes before I was spotted by one who ran off shortly to be followed by the other and we proceeded to the sett where we were pleased to see the first adult emerge at 7.07 from Zabbie's hole. Soon there were four adults (two pairs) grooming and scratching as a group. There was a great deal of scent, sufficient to overpower the stench of stinkhorn fungi on the woodland air. They were startled in by a bird flapping in the trees behind them and they stayed down until the woodland was quieter at about 7.45 when they resumed a peaceful evening. We were working our way back up over Aubrey's field when we turned to survey the scene.

There, wrestling and chasing on the far fields of the valley were the two fox cubs, dark and fair. We watched through field glasses until they romped down behind the trees and out of sight.

We did not see the fox cubs again that year but on August 8th, when we were returning from the sett at 8.00 pm. having seen the four adult badgers that were resident there, we saw a dog fox travelling across the far valley fields. He stopped to look in our direction before hurrying away. It seemed for all the world a kind of farewell.

We felt certain that the vixen had used part of the Brook Sett to raise her litter of cubs until sometime in June when they vacated the sett and moved to another den as they did in 1975, except in that year the move was enforced by the hostility of the badger community even though the vixen had triumphed in the fight that left blood and a dead badger.

Main Setts and Outliers.

The relevance of Aubrey's Sett to the colony at the Brook has for long been something of a mystery. As related Aubrey told us, often with disgust, when it was occupied by foxes for he did not approve. His attitude was coloured by the history of the local foxes assaulting his chickens; ours by the beauty of seeing them as an integral and indispensable part of the wildlife community of the valley. It was our habit to sit and wait in Aubrey's field in the hope of seeing a fox travelling across the valley and we often did, sometimes at close quarters but usually distant. We had been doing this one evening just as darkness was falling. We had not seen any foxes. Shortly after entering the lane we were startled by a voice from the gloom,

"Hello there."

When we gathered our shattered wits we could see that it was Aubrey stood perfectly still beneath a large oak, cradling in his arms a gun.

The barrel pointing to the sky. We knew at once that he had also been hoping to see a fox travelling and we were relieved to answer honestly his question,

"You seen any foxes down there for you tell me if you do?"

We knew that badgers from the Brook Sett visited Aubrey's for we had been able to track them as we did on the night of the hazelnut feast - a story we tell later.

51

We also witnessed this long suspected link in 1976. *July 19th.*

7.25 - A pair from Brook Sett. One made its way across the brook to disappear in the undergrowth of the bracken field.

We started for home but approached Aubrey's with caution. The same badger was there alone - our first positive observation of animals moving between the two setts.

From the map made in 1971 it can be seen that the setts are linked by well padded paths and the pattern of occupation suggests that it is a satellite or outlier sett used periodically by the badgers from the Brook Sett.

Ernest Neal uses the term outliers when dealing with the origin of setts and has this to say,

"When setts are formed, they are usually dug on existing territories as outliers of the main breeding sett. At first, they are only used spasmodically as alternative accommodation, but if one of these outliers is found to be suitable it may well be enlarged and eventually become another breeding sett."

This often happens in some communities, the badgers moving from one to another according to circumstances."

H. Mortimer Batten uses the term warren rather than sett and states that the animals never occupy the same warren for more than two or three months at a spell.

After which the warren is forsaken for a corresponding period to allow for complete sweetening. In the interim he suggests that the badger colony move themselves to another country residence, probably not more than a mile distant.

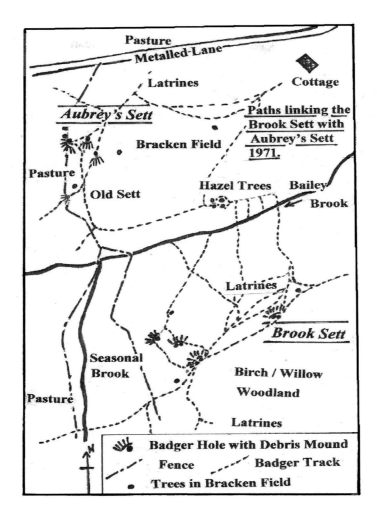

Howard Lancum describes the Devon sett he watched as occupied continuously for many years and goes on to say how difficult it is to persuade badgers to leave a sett altogether, except by using certain methods of his own!

The exact periods during which badgers use Aubrey's sett are difficult to isolate as foxes use and clean out the sett especially in September and October, leaving debris outside and giving all the signs of occupation. On the other hand the great extent of the digging out of the sett often suggests badgers at work and this has been confirmed by the evidence of their tracks.

At the Brook Sett occupation has been continuous over a number of years with foxes using part of it during the April/May/June period and all the resident badgers using it during the interesting July/August time when they behave as one large family. Based on this we believe that the Brook Sett is a main breeding sett and that Aubrey's is an outlier used periodically by the same colony of badgers as circumstances dictate.

To relate this to the observations of the quoted authorities
....

The Brook Sett is continuously occupied as 'Lancum' observed in Devon and Aubrey's Sett is subject to the periods of sweetening observed by Mortimer Batten.

Although routine excavation associated with sett cleaning goes on all year round only being noticeably reduced during November/December the peaks of activity are during February, April, and August-October.

These peaks are probably associated with important events in the badger calendar such as the birth of cubs and possibly the movement of the boar to separate quarters on the birth of cubs in Spring.

The Autumn peak is associated with preparation for winter and for expected cubs, and with the movement of one year old cubs into their own separate quarters.

Throughout the years when we were diligently keeping records of sett digging we often marvelled at the amount of debris deposited on mounds following a single night's work. Over time some mounds accumulated until they stood too high to see over and the badgers could only continue excavations by making a trench from the entrance through the mound to allow working on more level ground.

Some comparatively huge stones were thrown out and inevitably they rolled off the mound and accumulated near the base which became littered with stones up to five kilograms in weight. Sometimes it could be more aptly described as quarrying. At other times the debris was largely composed of used bedding scuffed out along with soil as the sleeping chambers were cleaned out. We were often tempted to consider a vertical profile cut through a mound - would it provide a visual history of activities at the sett?

By studying the layers and their contents perhaps it would be possible to ascertain the pattern of the past in terms of excavating new chambers, clearing out bedding and even excavating badger skeletons? However the dubious prospect of digging near a sett and its connotations put us off and that idea remains just a concept.

Many dead badgers must be interred in setts - we have found a large number of remains, usually being skulls or jaw bones, in the debris mounds of setts. We imagine that excavations have unearthed a skeleton interred perhaps years before and the remains have been dug from the sett and left with the other debris.

E.G. Neal in his book, 'Badgers', gives an excellent guide to establishing the age and sex of dead badgers from studying the skulls and he incorporates the work of Hancox on dentition and tooth wear to establish age.

Since we realised the viability of an ongoing study of excavated skulls we have used the guide to estimate the age and sex of skulls that come to our notice knowing that a prolonged study would reveal much useful information on the possible lifespan of badgers in the wild. We include two examples of notebook work done on skulls from the Brook Sett in 1981.

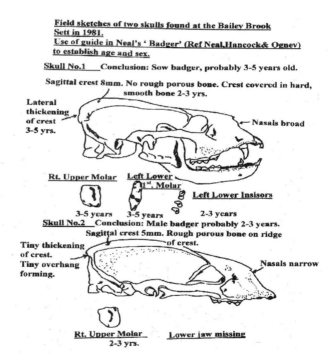

Field sketches of two skulls found at the Bailey Brook Sett in 1981.
Use of guide in Neal's ' Badger' (Ref Neal,Hancock& Ognev) to establish age and sex.

Skull No.1   Conclusion: Sow badger, probably 3-5 years old.

Sagittal crest 8mm. No rough porous bone. Crest covered in hard, smooth bone 2-3 yrs.

Lateral thickening of crest 3-5 yrs.

Nasals broad

Rt. Upper Molar   Left Lower 1st. Molar   Left Lower Insisors

3-5 years   3-5 years   2-3 years

Skull No.2   Conclusion: Male badger probably 2-3 years.

Sagittal crest 5mm. Rough porous bone on ridge of crest.

Tiny thickening of crest.
Tiny overhang forming.

Nasals narrow

Rt. Upper Molar   Lower jaw missing
2-3 yrs.

" Now don't forget any of this son .
There's the year we dug the stony chamber ~ see , all huge rocks ;
then the year they made hay in the top field so we changed the
beds every week and turned out so much stuff that outside was like
a bed as well ~ we slept there in the afternoon sun on some days
when it was safe .
And there is your Great Uncle Bawson's bones ~ of course he died
many years before that but that was the year we scuffed them out .
Before that is antiquity ."

**Lower jaw in debris. May 1974.
Brook Sett. Entrance M3.**

Femur bone. Local Sett

58

Skull - note sagittal crest. Local Sett.

Skull. May 1974. Brook Sett. Entrance M3.

Watching during April 1973 gave us our best opportunity to see badgers digging and quite a comical experience it was, prompting many a private chuckle as we later surveyed freshly excavated setts and recalled the events of that evening.

Saturday April 14th.
Weather - Day - heavy rain am, steady breeze, quite warm.
Evening - steady breeze in our faces, rising bright moon, sharp.
7.00 pm. - Arrived to watch Brook Sett. Woodpeckers in the canopy.
8.50 - Bumping noises underground - now poor light.
9.00 - A pair from M1 ducking in and out nervously.
9.20 - Seemed to go underground.

Decided to use a torch for the first time ever - we had fitted a red cellophane cover as we had heard that badgers cannot see red light - and were delighted to watch one badger working for 35 minutes to dig nine loads of soil and bedding. He paid no attention to the torchlight but broke off from digging several times to purr gently at the sett entrance.
He got no response and the nervous sow seen with him earlier did not come out until he had left when she hurried after him.

A magical moment when we knew that we had something special to look forward to - she had cubs below ground.

The boar excavated soil in a similar fashion to that employed for dragging in fresh bedding. Shuffling backwards he dragged the load of soil between his forepaws and tucked under his chin. When he reached the crest of the debris mound he scuffed the new load away between his back legs and down the slope.

Our amusement was caused by his comical reaction when stones rolled down the mound behind him. He looked startled and stared into the gloom to see what caused the noise, and when satisfied, he snorted and hurried back to work in the sett. This happened on each trip and the memory of a puzzled face staring at the rolling stones and then snorting in disgust epitomises for us the badger engaged on digging. As we left the brook that night the valley was bathed in bright light from the rising moon.

# Collection of Bedding.

Badgers collect material from above ground to use as a lining for their sleeping chambers. They gather up bundles of vegetation and tuck it under their chins clutching it between their forepaws just as for excavating. In this way the material is carried into the sett by shuffling backwards and dragging the ball along. Evidence of this work is often seen near setts and on the well padded paths established there. Bundles (balls) of bedding are often left on paths and near entrances. We have seen badgers prepare a bundle of bedding from vegetation near the sett and leave it where it was made, no doubt to be used at a later date. Very often the immediate sett area at the Brook is cropped bare where badgers have gathered up grass, bracken and foxglove for this purpose. As described earlier enormous amounts of bedding is collected in concentrated spells.

These seem to be confined to the period from June to September according to events recorded in the diaries. Very often green bedding is collected by actually cropping vegetation. This is done by the badgers flattening vegetation between their forepaws and then tearing it off. Grass and fern may be flattened with a sweep of the left forepaw followed by a sweep of the right. It is then torn off, with the more stubborn pieces being bitten through, before being transported back to the sett.

Throughout the year smaller amounts of bedding are gathered and we have quite frequently seen single bundles delivered during February and March by sow badgers who have emerged briefly and nervously only to collect bedding before disappearing below ground not to be seen again. We have taken this as further indication that cubs are present.

Whilst this cropping of green bedding is witnessed throughout most of the year the gathering of loose bedding is also common. Dry leaves are gathered and in August in particular, large quantities of freshly cut and dried hay have been carried a considerable distance from fields adjoining the Brook Sett copse.

'Howard Lancum' tells an amusing tale of how badgers took advantage of his efforts to build a hide from natural materials.

A hide made from a framework of tied branches covered in bracken and other soft materials was completely dismantled with a tell tale trail of its remains leading straight into the nearest hole. In an attempt to combat this he substituted the soft stuff with prickly gorse but that went too when, in February, he found several nearby holes stuffed full of gorse branches. 'Lancum' doubted the suitability of gorse at a time of the year when newly born cubs were present but 'Neal' confirms that gorse and even thistles are used during the winter months.

'Paget and Middleton' give examples of unusual materials being collected, such as the dry stalks of field beans which formed unwieldy bundles and potato tops which have not been sprayed prior to harvesting.

They also tell of setts in the coniferous woods of the North York Moors where only pine needles are readily available close to hand - the badgers have travelled hundreds of yards to gather more preferable material - so apparently there are limits.

The badgers at the Brook seem fortunately well endowed with suitable material close by for they crop the woodland slopes for fragrant bedding while those at Aubrey's take the springy bracken from their doorstep.

Only infrequently do they mount expeditions in search of other choice materials but it appears that some less fortunate animals will go to great lengths to furnish their chambers.

・Greater Spotted Woodpecker・
Brook Sett 14·4·73

Saturday 14 th. April 1973

7.00 pm. GMT. - A woodpecker is attacking a tree up on the side of the valley . There are a pair because one is behind us at the same time .

Strangely , one of the pair landed on the electricity pylon and bored that making a discordant metallic (LANG A LANG A LANG in the peace of the natural woodland sounds and the usual tap , tapping of woodpeckers on trees . However it appeared that no harm was done as the tapping continued until dusk at about 8.00 .

The instinctive urge to drill and bore must be great as they didn't learn (or if they did they didn't tell other woodpeckers) as this quite often happened and never failed to amuse . Amidst the calling and circling of the tawny owls , the cooing and flapping of the roosting wood pigeons and the chattering of woodmice on tree stumps it never seemed right somehow .

 # Food and Feeding.

The badger must be truly the most omnivorous of creatures for the list of foods it has been shown to take covers just about everything from mushrooms to fallen fruit, from wasp larvae to deer carcasses.

'Bradbury' assembled a comprehensive list of food remains found in dung samples collected from the Yorkshire region and he lists the following plant remains: grass, white clover, sorrel leaves, young buttercup shoots, oak and elm leaves, acorns, blackberries, windfall apples, plums, wheat, barley, oats, fungi, bracket fungi, morrel toadstools, tree roots, pignuts and coal fragments. As if that is not enough the animal remains identified were: the adult and larval stages of ground dwelling beetles (cockchafer grubs, wireworms, click beetles, dor beetles and ground beetles), caterpillars of moths, wasp and bumble bee nests.
Also centipedes, earwigs, spiders, millipedes, sawfly larvae, unweaned rabbits, woodmice, voles, rats (young and adult), hedgehogs, frogs, wild birds, deep litter fowl (taken from a refuse heap of dead birds), pheasant eggs (two samples only) and earthworms.

'Bradbury' points out that the diet is diverse and the animals adaptable!

Shortage of food is therefore unlikely to occur especially as survival in severe weather is probably ensured by seasonal weight changes, both boars and sows increasing in weight in the autumn and then using the accumulated fat reserves as an auxiliary energy supply in winter.

'Lancum' approached the discovery of the wild badger diet in a different way when in 1952 he experimented by laying foodstuffs on badger paths well away from the sett to test their attractiveness to badgers.

Honeycomb was avidly taken as were raw rabbits liver, sliced turnip, cockchafers, a mass of garden snails and fresh strawberries. Cooked potato was merely sampled and gorgonzola cheese, a smelly young rabbit, an unbroken hens egg and raw herring were rejected.

He also conducted an autumn experiment with fungi as food and found that mushrooms were readily taken as were Boletus edulis and Amanita rubescens but Amanita fulva and the poisonous species were not taken.

'Drabble' performed experiments with the food of tame badgers and confirmed that sweet things were taken first. His pet took bread and treacle, cake or anything with honey. Eggs were taken but meat and poultry were at the bottom of the list of preferences even when presented as a freshly killed hen still convulsing.

Out in the fields and woods it ate earthworms, beetles and larvae, slugs, voles and bluebell bulbs - it had to be kept out of the garden because of its liking for bulbs!

'Neal' reiterates that the badger is truly omnivorous saying that it will eat practically anything edible if it is hungry.

It is a forager rather than a hunter and although primarily an opportunist it does have preferences with earthworms right at the top of the list. It would hardly be possible to devise a diet and behaviour pattern causing less conflict with man's interests than that of the badger.

Without a shadow of doubt one of the most exciting watches we made at the Brook Sett was in July 1973.

It was to do with food. Our attention had been absorbed by two shrews one of which had tiptoed across the nearest mound and picked its way down to our left into a decaying woodpile and the other which foolishly lingered near the sett entrance rummaging about at the base of a sapling.

Saturday 14th July
Weather - Day - cooler, rain during afternoon. Evening –
No rain, damp air and cooler. No breeze, fog later.

6.50 - Arrived at sett.
7.00 - Hollow thumps underground.
7.05 - One dishevelled cub (with ragged tail) from Zabbie's hole - good light. His reaction was predictable as he picked up the scent of the first shrew and heard the shrill squeaking of the second. With businesslike urgency he sprang around to locate the prey, he was tense, alert and powerful, poising himself for the strike. Stabbing the ground with his forepaws, power surging from his arched back, he tossed the shrew into the air, lost it, found it, played with it and bit it until it was dead, an opportunist meal taken by a creature who was magnificent, savage and truly wild.

In August 1977 we were fortunate to wait only forty minutes to see badgers

Wednesday 10th.

Weather - Day - very hot, dry. Evening - Hot, still and dry.

6.45 - Arrived at sett.

7.45.-.Three adults from Zabbie's hole. An hour spent watching them scratching, grooming, squabbling playfully and feeding. One of them took a snail from the path. Fastidious manner as it cracked the shell and held it down with its forepaws while it extracted the body from the broken pieces. Quite a spectacle to highlight the evening.

The long list of foods used to illustrate the wide omnivorous diet of the badger did not mention hazelnuts but 1976 presented us with a further chance to see badgers feeding when the fare was more plentiful as we witnessed what has become known as 'The Hazelnut Feast.'

September 20th.

Watching at the Brook Sett in a position which allowed us to see across the steep sided valley to the slopes of the bracken field near Aubrey's.

5.55 - One badger from the Brook Sett to make its way across the valley to the bracken field.

- Used field glasses to watch it foraging around some hazel bushes. Loud crunching and cracking as it enjoyed its meal of nuts.

The badger moved from one hazel bush to the next for forty-five minutes feasting on fallen nuts before it disappeared from view and hearing.

We crept up on it at Aubrey's Sett on the way home.

69

Electricity cables pass directly overhead from the pylon which stands some thirty yards North East of the Brook Sett and in 1972 the taller birch and willow were fouling the cables. In November workmen moved in to clear the offending timber but they left the fallen branches exactly where they fell blocking sett entrances and cluttering paths.

In December the work looked finished and I decided to move the timber into piles to clear the sett area. We wanted to help the badgers and ensure that our watching positions still afforded a clear view of the sett.

We had noticed that old piles of logs, now rotting, were a popular feeding spot and new piles may afford a food source in years to come.

This indeed proved to be the case for by 1982 two of the three piles were regularly visited by badgers foraging for food.

They claw off the decaying bark and break up the softening wood, seeking insects.

We mention 1982 because in that year we had to repeat the clearance operation following powerline work.

The aspect of the sett location appears to have some bearing on the badgers feeding habits in severe weather. This was especially noticeable in January 1974 when we made specific mention of it in our diary.

The bank on which the Brook Sett lies is north facing and severe frosts do not thaw readily as the sun does not shine on it. The opposite bank of the valley, where Aubrey's Sett lies, is south facing and soon thaws.

On New Year's Eve 1973 a hard frost froze the valley sides and by January 3rd. the Brook side had not thawed for three days.

The south facing Aubrey's Sett had thawed each day and it was apparent that the badger colony had moved to that side for feeding as a large area had been churned up by rooting. Of course there was no evidence of rooting on the frozen north facing side.

Rooting is the term used to describe badgers foraging for food either in the turf of pasture land or in the loose leaf litter of the woodland floor.

The larvae and adult forms of ground dwelling beetles, earthworms and roots and bulbs are discovered in this way. In pastureland the badger scrapes a small hole with its paws and then thrusts in its nose which appears a very tight fit.

We presume that nibbling, sucking and licking extracts the food the badger is seeking.

It is common to see badgers work their body around part of a circle whilst keeping their nose buried in the rooting spot. In loose leaf litter the nose is often sufficient without use of the claws to make a hole and foraging badgers may be seen literally up to their ears in leaf litter or soft soil. The holes left behind are sometimes referred to as snuffle holes or rooting spots - the results of intensive work leaving patches of ground churned up to an amazing extent.

When colleagues, neighbours and friends learn of your interest in badgers they invariably relate some tale of badgers in their district. In this way we have been able to glean smidgeons of information. One such tale was related to me when we lived at Salisbury, Wiltshire.

It might well be entitled The Strawberry Growers Lament for it told of a gardener who was fond of all forms of wildlife, especially badgers, but whose affection was being tested to its limits by the local badgers who were decimating his prized and valuable strawberry crop.

He had a large strawberry bed which he was attempting to build into a significant enterprise to provide seasonal income but every night badgers were consuming large quantities of the succulent ripe strawberries.

Having seen the culprits he described them as like troopers storming some bastion of resistance, arriving in great numbers and attacking in waves. He did not want to harm the badgers but this could no longer be tolerated and he was reduced to entertaining the distasteful option of shooting them. What other measure should he try before resorting to that?

We advised two things - first peg a creosote soaked rope around the bed just above the ground and stop any holes in hedges with creosote rags. This may deter the animals.

Secondly, find the setts and stop the holes with more creosote rags, in an effort to drive them away.

The report came back that the first measure had been tried but the badgers had just galloped over the intended barricade and he would try the second but privately we doubted that the badgers would be denied such rich pickings and the last we heard they were still taking their share. Of course our advice would be different now given the new methods and technologies available for dissuasion.

Climbing and Scratching.

The trees that grow near the mounds thrown out of the Brook Sett are willow and entrance M1 used to have one growing right out of its mound because the debris had accumulated around it so much.

Unfortunately this particular tree was felled to prevent it fouling the overhead power cables but for years it had featured as a favourite scratching and playing tree for successive families of badgers.

The fallen play tree.

Even after the felling operations the stumps were used as playthings by the cubs and this and other willows nearby became deeply scarred sometimes up to a height of twelve feet, this high altitude work being attributed to the abundant grey squirrel population.

The lower level scratching was undoubtedly the work of badgers using the trees as scratching posts to clean their claws.

In July 1971 we had been watching a group of six badgers cleaning and scratching themselves on a close, thundery evening when a cub reached up to scratch the M1 willow to a height of three to four feet but he did not climb off the ground. More was seen in June 1974 ....

Saturday 22nd.

Weather - Day - very hot, still. Evening - warm, still, quarter moon.

7.30 GMT. Arrived at Brook Sett. Badgers already out at M4/M5 relaxed as if out for some time. Total of nine seen in at least two families - much play and wrestling. Cubs using polished fallen tree trunk as a balancing beam - running from one end to the other. Adult lifted himself up a tree to a height of about four feet clinging on in bear like fashion.

This was the only time we ever saw a badger climbing and it was a feature of play rather than seeking food.

We were fascinated to read in Neal's 'Badgers' that the wolverine (Gulo gulo) which is a near relative of the badger marks trees near its den by repeated biting and chewing and that this marking may act as a scent marker of territorial significance. We realised that we had seen badgers biting or chewing repeatedly at the same tree stump, root or other obvious landmark within their territory.

In June 1982 we had watched several times when three badgers, two adults and a cub, left M3 to move straight to the valley of the seasonal tributary brook. We saw them for about thirty seconds and they were gone.

We had enjoyed some success at following the badgers from place to place, carefully circling clear of the sett and reapproaching where we thought they would be. This we did and, sure enough, they were foraging just along the path they had taken but were returning slowly towards the sett. The path is so well padded that it must be in very regular use and at one point it passes an overhanging tree stump. This landmark is very obvious as the path deviates to pass it.

The badgers stopped to chew at this stump and further investigation has shown it to be very well gnawed.

It is quite possible that they were leaving a scent marker especially as it became a routine for badgers to emerge and go straight to the latrines above the sett before returning to spend more time playing and grooming near the sett.

Routine visits to latrines are thought to be important as territorial marking systems, perhaps gnawing is significant too.

Further evidence of scratching at trees came in a round about fashion as a result of our efforts to photograph the badgers at the Brook and may also serve as evidence of the animals' curiosity about their environment.

We had been trying to take photographs using a two inch reflector flash but discovered that as soon as they saw the reflector they retreated in alarm. In an attempt to overcome this difficulty we embarked on an experiment. We cut two inch circles of silver foil and pinned them to various trees in the vicinity of the sett at about the height that the reflector would be when it was mounted on the camera and tripod.

We hoped the badgers would investigate the circles, find them harmless, and so be less alarmed at the real thing. We first tried this in late January.

January 31st 1971.

Placed silver foil on trees in preparation for photography.

February 20th. Silver foil circles gone without trace. Pinned new circles on trees.

March 6th.

Foil circles from outside M1 clawed and partly missing, later found torn and screwed up in a rooting spot under nearby holly bush. Replaced circle.

March 27th. Foil circles missing. Scratch marks where one had been. Shredded foil found in rooting spots.

The badgers had indeed investigated and scratched down our mock reflectors. They were not then alarmed by the real reflector as long as we kept it still.

We tried two systems for photography - set up the camera and flash on a tripod and focus it for a picture where we thought badgers would be, then retreat to cover and trigger the shutter with an air release mechanism should they oblige. This worked sometimes but we found it much better to hold the camera and wait to see where badgers actually were. In general the click or the flash or both startled the badgers and too often getting a photograph ended the evenings watching with them hiding underground.

It seemed you were either a watcher or a photographer and it was difficult to pair the two. We always resisted the temptation to place down food bait to bring the badgers to a desired spot for a picture.

A close friend once observed that we visited them so often that the badgers would soon be tame and we winced at the thought for we wanted to observe them in the genuinely wild and natural state. Our thinking was a bit purist in that respect.

Mating and Family Life.

Current opinion confirms that mating between badgers can take place at any time during the year but observers distinguish between short term (maybe just a form of play) and long term mating which only occurs when the sow is in full oestrus and so leads to fertilisation. Observations of long term mating are spread well across the year as the incidence of sows coming into full oestrus is governed by several interrelated issues such as the maturity, the date of birth of the last litter born and the stage of lactation for any particular sow, but Neal's data suggests three peak periods for long duration mating, in February, April/Early May and September, and that these peaks may coincide with sows being in full oestrus.

It is well known that badger sows are the subject of delayed implantation and whilst mating may well take place at any time the cubs are normally born at one season only.

The fertilised egg forms a blastocyst which does not implant in the uterus in the usual way but remains alive and free within the uterus for a variable period of time before becoming implanted in the uterus wall when it is appropriate. This appropriate time appears to be during the period of reduced activity during December which allows for approximately two months of traditional gestation before the cubs are born in February.

We have previously mentioned mating taking place in May when it lasted for less than a minute despite the boar and sow indulging in a lot of purring of an affectionate nature prior to his brief mounting.

We have also witnessed brief matings in May, June and July but the diary terms them playful attempts as they have been short lived (less than two minutes) and penetration was doubtful.

On one occasion in May a more determined attempt was witnessed when the boar mounted the sow following a considerable spell of playing and wrestling which could have been mistaken for fighting.

The boar tried to keep the sow in position by biting her ear but she resisted and we thought it unsuccessful although the official expression short term mating could have been used.

It was July 1973 when we first witnessed long duration mating and that was sadly interrupted by a sudden unaccountable alarm which sent all the badgers underground in haste.

Friday 27th. July.

Weather - Day - hot, clear, still. Evening - clear, very light breeze.

7.10 GMT. - Arrived at Brook Sett

7.20 - First badger from new hole behind our position. By 7.30 there are five all from this hole - much scratching and communal grooming.

7.35 - Two left in the direction of the stream.

7.50 - Mating - the boar mounted a sow biting the back of her neck when she tried to move away - caused her to squeal and yelp - she was held for several minutes. Then he sat back and licked her genitals.

This sequence was repeated a number of times - the third badger watched unperturbed from the entrance well. Sudden alarm sent them in - no sign of them for some time. We left in good light.

This proved to be the latest date when mating was witnessed and it was never seen amongst the Brook badgers outside the period from May to July covered by the incidents described here.

Assuming that fertilisation was achieved during the May - July mating activity the sequence of events leading up to the birth of the cubs must allow for a period of delayed implantation until the appropriate time in December followed by the requisite two months of traditional gestation, and then a further eight - ten weeks before the diligent watcher might expect to see cubs making their first appearances above ground.

'Neal' gives three diagrams to explain the sequence as governed by the time of fertilisation and the diagram from our notebook, shown here, would apply to the Brook badgers given the circumstances described above.

Having witnessed mating in May - July 1973 we determined to make special efforts to follow the progress of the colony in 1974. Accordingly we made the first successful watch of the year in February. ....

Sunday 17th.

The Brook is a noisy torrent following a very wet spell.

5.30 – Arrived for first watch of year.

6.25 - One from Zabbie's hole, not cautiously, to collect one bundle of bedding nearby and return below ground. Thumping noises as it was taken below us to Ladder hole or M1 chambers.

6.50 - We left in poor light having seen or heard
nothing more. Owls over the valley.

Similar behaviour to this in other years - collection of bedding, not leaving the sett area - had been associated with cubs being present or imminent and we were hopeful this time.

Daytime visits on 18th. February and 17th. March showed little excavation, just a scattering of fresh soil from M1b, M3 and S1 but several holes with tell tale trails of bedding being taken in. In March the area suffered an eight inch fall of snow accompanied by very cold conditions.

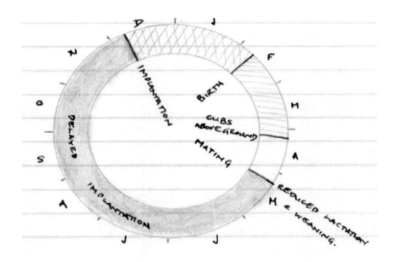

We made a watch on March 16th. from 5.40 to 7.00 but left cold, wet and uncomfortable having seen nothing. By the end of March weather conditions had improved considerably.

....

Sunday 31st.

Weather - Day - very warm, sunny day. Evening - clear, still cold later, bright half moon.

6.30 - Arrived.

7.05 - Noises underground

7.25 - First badger from Ladder hole

7.35 - Two from M4 region into Zabbie's hole - some bedding collected but not taken in - some scratching - affectionate nuzzling - stayed near the sett going in and out.

Once again we thought this hesitant behaviour suggested cubs underground that could not be left unguarded for long.

April saw similar outdoor conditions and watches revealed a colony ill at ease, nervously darting in and out, but busy with fresh deep red sandy soil spilling from seven of the holes onto the spring carpet of oxalis, anemone, stitchwort, bluebell and golden saxifrage. Underground noise was increasing.

By May 11th. The noises had developed into squealing and yickering and we thought the cubs had ventured out at S1 although we did not see them. That pleasure was delayed until late May...........................

Sunday 26th

Weather - Day - hot, still, dry. Evening - overcast, warm, breezy.

7.20 - Settled at Brook Sett - male bullfinch in low canopy.

7.45 - Owls.

8.00 - Muffled noises underground.

8.05 - One to sniff at Zab's. But did not emerge.

8.20 - One male adult from Zab's. to M4 - two faces at hole - another adult left - more faces - meanwhile two adults in and out of Ladder hole and M4.

Then, mother and two cubs from Zab's. - boisterous - heard yickering in woods after they left. From M2 one boar then one cub (small, fluffy, grey) trotted after the others - these groups hesitant to mix - boar from Ladder started on path but turned back on seeing mother and cubs.

8.45 - All quiet - strong musky smell on air - we left.

On May 28th emergence was preceded by a long spell of faces appearing at various holes to sniff the air cautiously. One adult eventually emerged from the Ladder hole soon to be followed by a group of one adult and three cubs. A great deal of coming and going with cubs racing back and forth to the woodland defied a count of heads.

We were back on May 31st. to witness a routine often seen when cubs are present. The boar emerged to tour the sett area (he often tours the woodland adjacent to the sett as well) and then visit Zab's. hole to call out the cubs with a low purring sound. Mother and three cubs came out and we watched the complete family group of five until we left them still engrossed in their play.

Interestingly Neal comments that in a typical year when cubs are born early in February the boar is kept away from the nest chamber by the sow.

Usually he emerges first and trots from hole to hole and over the whole area of the sett making deep, vibrant, whinnying purrs almost continuously. His whinnying suggests that he is trying to call up the sow, but the wider patrolling of the area seems to be of territorial significance.

Frequent watches during June saw this family together until on the 22nd. there seemed to be nine badgers present in all. Other watches full of mutual grooming, purring, yickering and playing revealed six cubs amongst the adults at the Brook Sett. Things clarified a little on July 21st

Sunday 21st.

Weather - Day - very hot, sunny, still. Evening - warm with breeze.

6.40 - Arrived at Ladder hole watch.

6.47 - Badgers from M1 region to M4 region - two adults and three cubs plus two adults and two cubs - two distinct families.

7.30 - One from Ladder hole - very cautious - finally left at 8.10.

This was a positive identification of two separate families, but still other badgers seemed to be present.

We remembered our watching of 1971 when it became a feature to wait for a cautious adult after the others had gone. We thought that the same situation might prevail in 1974 and we deduced the colony to comprise of six cubs, three belonging to one family and two to a separate family which left one cub.

This lone cub, we believed, belonged to the nervous adult that stayed at the sett after the others had gone, joining infrequently in their activities.

The total number in residence was eleven and they lived as a community until September with adults and cubs from different families intermixing freely.

Aubrey's Sett was reoccupied in September with debris, soil, stones and bedding being cleared out and the bracken field being cropped for fresh bedding. The community at the Brook had split up and some of them moved to use Aubrey's as winter quarters or at least as temporary accommodation before settling for the winter.

As we have so frequently observed, when badgers first emerge from their setts they often sit in the shallow depression formed by the entrance and indulge in a thoroughly communal grooming session.

In using the term grooming we differentiate between individual badgers scratching and cleaning themselves and the process of grooming where groups of badgers work on each others coats by nibbling and cleaning the fur.

Badgers do shake themselves vigorously and scratch furiously just after emerging for the first time in an evening but communal or mutual grooming is less common and appears to be so appreciated by all the participants that it is accompanied by the smell of musk scent.

A characteristic pose for two badgers grooming is adopted when each badger nibbles the back of the other's neck by standing head on and sliding the head past its partners head to reach around to the nape of the neck so that the heads appear intertwined.

They also lie down and work all over each other's flanks with the same nibbling and cleaning actions.

We have seen this mostly in the spring and summer months and especially when communal living is in full swing. It is apparently a process which aids familiarisation and acceptance between members of a social group.

Observations of grooming behaviour in other species of animals that live in herds, packs or colonies have led to similar conclusions.

Maurice Burton says that social exchanges are not uncommon among such animals and, in his writing about the dusky footed wood rat of North America, he interestingly describes grooming as they groom each other, male grooms female and vice versa; adults groom the young, the young groom the adults and each other. It is carried out by a rapid nibbling and pawing of the whole body, the teeth passing rapidly through the fur and touching the skin, the individual being groomed rolling over to facilitate the efforts of the one performing the operation.

Grooming can therefore be identified as part of the establishment of a social bond.

Hugo and Jane van Lawick-Goodall write about grooming in golden jackals. They point out that grooming, in many creatures, has become an important affair socially and, as well as serving to cleanse the fur, may also help to strengthen affectionate ties within the group, or cement the relationship between males and females during courtship.

Grooming undoubtedly has this function in golden jackal society. Although there is no proven link between the grooming habits of these other species and those of the badger the observations may be of value in evaluating the significance of mutual grooming in badgers.

Neal suggests that it appears to have a social function in badgers and his report of John Sankey's description of a badger grooming by running the teeth over the surface, the hair being drawn between the teeth but with no attempt to bite is similar to the description of wood rats

The many instances of grooming amongst the badgers at the Brook Sett confirm its importance as a social behaviour and feature of family life supplemented by other examples of recognition and acceptance

Saturday 8th. July

Weather - Day - warm and still. Evening - hot, dry clear, still.

7.05 - Arrived.

7.20 - First badger from Zab's hole - a cub - then yickering and yelping underground for five - ten minutes. Adult from new hole behind us - met cub on the path - sniffed and nuzzled the cub rubbing its face with her snout before both returned underground.

They knew each other!

Persecution.

Picture this scene if you can. Four men crowd around a badger sett in a secluded Forest of Dean woodland glade armed with a spade and a long metal bar. They have dug into the sett until a badger has been isolated and forced above ground by the terriers that accompany the excited gathering. The pack of dogs numbers eight in all and they have set upon the badger which bears the marks of battle. It is splattered with blood on its shoulders and back but has defended itself fiercely leaving savage bites on two lurcher dogs and one of the terriers with its jaw hanging off its mouth. The savagery is halted by a sympathetic man who rushes onto the scene waving a stick to break up the shouting, snarling, barking melee, and the terrified badger takes its chance to find safety underground. If asked to put a date to the incident would you guess at probably the 18th century for a scene of such cruelty and barbarity? Perhaps details of a second incident will give more clues?

Three men are observed climbing over a gate in company with six terriers. They are armed with two chains, four spades and a crowbar. The observers' attention has been drawn by the sound of voices and the yelping of dogs coming from the woodland. One of the dogs is covered in blood. The observer is a police sergeant who challenges the men to explain their actions.

Looking for foxes is the explanation but further investigation reveals a freshly dug hole with splashes of blood.

The carcass of a recently killed badger is unearthed and one of the men admits, after questioning, that he killed the badger with a spade when it would not release its hold on one of the dogs. No it is not the 18th. Century, it is 1975. (Incident one) and 1979 (Incident two) and the details of this gruesome entertainment are only readily available because both incidents resulted in prosecutions under the 1973 Badgers Act and resulted in fines totalling £100 and £150 respectively, the proceedings being reported in the local press.

Sidney Williams writing in the Daily Mirror of August 7th. 1972 says that badger digging is (at that date) a national sport. Like cockfighting used to be. Or bear baiting. Clubs exist in every county - particularly in the North of England - where the local bully boys go out armed with a Jack Russell terrier and a handful of shovels and tear the badgers out of their homes with tongs.

Once out the diggers either kill the badger with the shovel or turn him wounded over to the Jack Russell. It gives the dogs "a bit of fun." Williams goes on to say that at that time there was nothing illegal about badger digging. But now it, and other forms of persecution against badgers and their environments, are illegal.

Protection was first afforded by the 1973 Badgers Act which came into force on 25th January 1974 and has been reviewed, strengthened and amended since to provide further measures.

H.M.S.O. publications and many books offer readers a full account of the protection currently provided but unfortunately it all came too late for the badgers of a beautifully situated sett in the region of the Brook badgers.

Ironically the nearest settlement is called Brockweir and it was horrified relatives living there who reported the persecution of March 1970 when no law afforded any protection to the badgers and nothing legal could have been done had we arrived in time.

But we heard that the diggers had "two badgers dead out on the bank," and the horrible scene of destruction they left behind was a serious setback at a time when we were beginning our quest to see and know wild badgers.

We photographed the gaunt hollows left under the shade of the mature canopy of birch and ash where a once picturesque sett had been and through the viewfinder we saw dark trenches etched in eerie shades of blue and grey where we should have seen rich brown soil spilling onto the verdant green carpet of the woodland floor speckled with the gay colours of the first flowers of spring. ....

Once again our resolve was strengthened to do something to promote love for wild and beautiful things and in particular under-standing of the fine stoic and vibrant creatures we have come to know.

We hope this shines through what we have written here and makes more people feel like this........

Watching by Ben Childs February 1990
~ Aged 15 years.

'We set off, my father and I, on the short walk into the woods, past the odd hole that we assume was a bees nest dug up by the animal that we intend to see, the badger. We come out of the woods and cross the recently replanted clearing, down the Forestry Commission track and then cut across another clearing heading for the sett.'

'When we arrive, just as dusk is beginning to creep across the sky, we locate the sett, check the direction that the wind is blowing and settle ourselves downwind. Badgers have a very keen sense of smell and will not appear if they sense the presence of danger. Whilst watching you must make as little noise as possible, the badgers' hearing is almost as good as its smell.'

'Once you are positioned in front of or beside a natural object the waiting begins.'

'A badger's eyesight is reasonably poor. Because it is nocturnal it has little or no use for good eyesight. Its eyes are good enough, however, to recognise a change to its skyline, a foreign silhouette, especially a moving one, will be recognised as a threat thus impairing your chances of seeing these beautiful creatures.'

'I personally do not mind the waiting, so long as you are warm and reasonably comfy you can stay still for quite a long time.'

'Being still means that you get to not only see the badgers, but also a host of other nocturnal animals, owls, bats and mice are the most common things, but on a good night you may also get to see foxes and occasionally a deer may pass you by.'

'Then a long, slender nose appears over the mound of excavated earth, this rotates around the entrance, then the head appears, ears pricked, ever ready to pick up the slightest sound and send the badger scurrying back into its hole. When the animal is satisfied that no danger is present it will emerge, staying close to the entrance for a few moments and then moving silently into the night. Shortly after the appearance of the first badger a second will appear, then a third and so on until the whole family has emerged.'

'I like these outings with my father because I like the peace and quiet of the woods at night; everything looks different when under the influence of moonlight. I see badger watching as a challenge; it tests your patience and ability to go unnoticed. For me, the reward for seeing these shy and peaceful creatures is the satisfaction of knowing that they are all right. And being able to keep track of the social goings on within the group.'

'I enjoy walking to and from the setts, especially at night, everything is quiet, the air is crisp and you seem to be the only living things on earth. Badgers are being unnecessarily persecuted by people known as badger baiters. This is illegal, but the punishments for those that are caught are so inadequate that many reassume their bloodthirsty habits almost immediately.'

"Badgers need all the friends they can get."

Persecution can take many forms, digging and baiting being two that affect badgers. Another is the manner in which they have been targeted for extermination campaigns because it is suspected that they comprise a reservoir in wildlife for a disease which affects cattle and their dairy products - tuberculosis.

The culling of badgers in an attempt to investigate or rather to prove a point has seen the slaughter of thousands regardless of whether they were infected and suffering or perfectly healthy, and the manner in which they have been dispatched has sometimes been found to be at worst cruel and at best suspect because of the suffering it may have caused.

However, mulling over what has been and is being done can achieve nothing unless we can stand back, encourage reasoned thought and reflection, and so hope to lend weight to another solution.

When you try to consider the issue of Tuberculosis in Cattle and Badgers the debate can quickly become a conflict of emotions ranging from livelihood of farmers and the humane treatment of domesticated animals through to conservation of wildlife and the production of wholesome dairy foods for the nation.

Reasonable decisions can be clouded by the whole gamut of emotions and by obdurate opinions on one or other of the very real threats presented by the issue.

Some clarity may be achieved by laying down a few ground rules for the discussion - scientifically valid statements which underpin a wide variety of opinions and views and give the lie to others ground rules like:

- living things suffer from illnesses and diseases which they encounter in their environments,

- disease in wild populations tends to be controlled naturally. Certain individuals have immunity which allows them to remain strong and healthy; they breed and pass on their immunity to future generations while sickly individuals die off. A process which ensures the viability of the species,

- artificially high populations of domesticated animals are especially vulnerable to whatever diseases they encounter. The density of the populations lends itself to communicating the disease to others,

– artificially high and domesticated populations. (e.g. dairy cattle confined by farm boundaries) need careful management because disease cannot be allowed to run its natural course for financial reasons, the health of the population is paramount to the production of wholesome food and to profitable farming businesses,

– wild populations tend to control the movement of groups and individuals between groups by a system of territories dominated by fit, strong, healthy individuals. This has an impact on the spread of disease as the unhealthy and weak are crowded out.

The implications of these ground rules are that wild animals in the countryside have evolved the potential to handle disease and illness in their ranks. Artificially high populations of domesticated animals have not evolved this potential at a level which embraces man's financial and food production needs. Neither of the two populations, wild or domesticated, can handle interaction between them without managed assistance of their environments. This is especially true where disease control is concerned. This essential management of environments can take several forms.

The domesticated animal populations must have their movement and contact with others organised for them by restricted movement or non-contact with diseased animal groups or individuals. Protection against disease is another aspect of this management and medicines and vaccines are one feature of the veterinary care the animals need.

The problems caused when disease is communicated between populations as when cattle infect badgers with tuberculosis, or badgers infect cattle, or both, are the subject of very contentious decisions. There seems little remaining doubt that both the badger and cattle suffer from tuberculosis and that they probably pass the disease between them.

It seems that live cattle can be diagnosed with tuberculosis but badgers cannot, so where badgers are suspected of communicating tuberculosis to cattle one measure has been to slaughter and remove all the badgers or at least all those which encounter the cattle. In fairness it should be understood that all the cattle which may have been exposed to infection are destroyed and removed as well.

However this presents problems as the badgers tend to move in and occupy any territory left vacant by destroyed badgers, and of course, farms need to restock with new cattle if they are to continue in the dairy business.

The debate seems to be gelling into a major question - is the wholesale slaughter of badgers acceptable as a means of protecting the dairy cattle population?
Or, is the wholesale slaughter of cattle acceptable as a means of protecting the badger population? To satisfy the emotions and needs of all interested parties the answer to both sides of the question must be no! So what can be done?

Again, any solution may depend on all concerned accepting a few ground rules...........
~ Where animals are kept in artificially high populations their keepers must take extraordinary measures to combat the spread of disease by its natural mechanisms.

This is valuable, even essential work - the production of food for the nation. The Ministry of Agriculture, Fisheries and Food have made available advice on the management of dairy herds to avoid cross contamination with badgers (M.A.F.F. 2000 & 2001) but farmers cannot be expected to manage such a fundamental move against the rules of natural evolution without help, especially if they are to make a profitable living from dairy farming and keep their product at a reasonable price.

The need to produce food from artificially high populations of domesticated livestock must be paid for by grants and finances to overcome 'natural' losses.

And it is; losses are compensated; but is enough done to ensure that all the recommended M.A.F.F. measures are financed and implemented?

There are implications for the farmer in labour costs, education costs and equipment costs. Can we afford not to make this work compulsory with herds that suffer tuberculosis breakdown, and in turn finance the farmers' efforts centrally so that the cost of milk production does not spiral out of control?

~ The wild and domesticated livestocks cannot be expected to respond to artificially high densities of population without help to overcome the 'natural' spread of disease.

Vaccination and medication are two alternatives to slaughter. The wholesale slaughter of anything that is vulnerable to suffering from or communicating disease is a brutal and blinkered response to the problem. And of course it has not been the only response - vaccines to immunise the badger from tuberculosis infection have been developed.

There are however, some problems with their effective use - has a sufficient proportion of the available funds been directed at the effort to explore this solution - have enough research projects been funded to expedite and further this work or has elimination of the source of infection via slaughter dominated our response? Even if the tenuous possibility that badgers are not a wildlife reservoir for tuberculosis in cattle proves to be the case, surely the fact that two significant living populations – badgers and cattle - are suffering from disease is justification enough for more research into medical solutions?

If progress is to be made towards a solution that is acceptable to all interested parties then time, effort and finances need to be directed at the following areas, and the parties need to be informed and reassured that this is being done ....

- helping the badger population eliminate disease by researching, developing and administering vaccines and medicines for them,

- helping the badger population by developing a live test to diagnose tuberculosis in wild living badgers so that culling can become selective with only those infected with the disease and their immediate contacts being destroyed.

Incidentally it was the ability to do just this with cattle that enabled tuberculosis in cattle to be brought largely under control in the first half of the twentieth century up to 1960 and which, ever since then, has been used to monitor herds for tuberculosis infection and so prevent the disease being communicated to people via contaminated milk; something that was a severe threat in the early nineteen hundreds. This success story for cattle from the past may yet be a way forward for badgers in the future!

– helping the domesticated livestock population by researching, developing and administering vaccines and medicines for them,

– helping the domesticated livestock population by providing them with an environment in which disease is less and less likely to be communicated to and among them.

The killing of living things to alleviate their suffering should be but one small strand of the solution to this complex problem.

A WIDER VIEW.

Digging beneath the surface.

In his book 'Geology Explained in the Forest of Dean and Wye Valley' William Dreghorn describes a geological journey down the River Wye and he has this to say about the Lower Wye Valley ....

'.......there is a rapid change of scene on the left bank of the river at Brockweir, where there is another kind of natural amphitheatre known as Hewelsfield Common. Here the steep walls of the Wye gorge give way to a more subdued relief, so that we have numerous small cottages perched all over the hills overlooking the valley.'

'This more open section of the Wye gorge is due to the presence of numerous faults in the Upper Devonian rocks (Tintern Sandstone Group).'

'The outcrop of these softer strata occurs over a wider area resulting in fewer sharper features of relief and more arable land.'

The description rings a bell ....

.........sandy stratum immediately below the hard carboniferous limestone/the exploitation of soft strata with hard impermeable overlays/well drained soils in lias sands and limestone rubble over sands (grassland and woodland)/the type of country which is hilly, has a sandy soil and contains a high proportion of deciduous woodland interspersed with fertile grassland containing a high density of earthworms, (Neal E.G. 1977) These details drawn from the investigation of the preferred environment of badgers match so precisely to the geological description that they go a long way towards explaining why this is badger country.

Just as Dreghorn suggests the area is a broad valley of predominantly Tintern Sandstone with significant outcrops of Quartz Conglomerate and Brownstones (mainly sandstone) in the valley floor.

The higher ground marking the perimeter of the amphitheatre is limestone giving way to Lower Dolomite. And, as Neal and his consultants anticipate, the badgers have exploited the geology and the land formations in locating their setts. The area has many setts in woods and copses, in hedgerows and in pasture but the established and ancient breeding ones occur where the softer Tintern Sandstone meets overlying limestones, where Lower Limestone Shales meet Quartz Conglomerate and where Tintern Sandstone meets Lower Limestone Shales.

There are subsidiary or outlier setts in the sandstone of the valley floor but they have not been developed past seasonal occupation and obviously do not meet the rigorous specifications required, which we will discuss briefly later.

Our regular walks in the area of the amphitheatre of the Common with its valley and brook in its bubbling youth and meandering maturity; with its rugged ridges and puddingstone field walls; its sun drenched south facing slope sprinkled with cottages and farms and its cool north facing wilderness fields allowed us to visit all the setts and keep notes of the wider picture of the badger population.

A typical diary entry for such a walk comes from August 1982..............

Daytime visit to all setts.

Brook Sett - clearing of tall timber from power lines has admitted more light.
Badgers seem to be moving down the bank into more cover (ladder hole, etc.) and around into the seasonal brook (two new holes). Latrines are under the hazel bushes on the north side of the brook, under the dead hazel above the sett, and near the elms and oaks at the top of the wood under the limestone cliffs. Collected soil and rock samples.

Aubrey's Sett 1

Reoccupied on 24th. August: first excavation of this year: is the colony at the Brook breaking up? No bedding taken in. Blank watch on 24.08.82 - 7 ~ 9.30 pm.

Aubrey's Sett 2

Still a single hole in the wall of the old cart track. Mound bare of vegetation. We know badgers made this because Aubrey told us so (opened late 1971).

Sunny Sett

In use not much fresh digging but badger tracks in soft mud. Holes in pasture field reopened.

Ridge Sett

Not occupied very overgrown except one hole onto the top ridge field.

New Sett

Single hole in hedgerow. Not used for some years. Mound indistinct.

Sandy Sett

Occupied. Some fresh digging but largely unchanged.

Jim's Sett

Beautiful sett - fully occupied - digging from several holes - scratch marks in polished play logs - bare patches around play trees - scratching of trees - tracks in dust - huge latrines full of layers of dung showing repeated use - clear path into woods to east and south. There is a distinct seasonal brook nearby, very similar to the landscape at the Brook Sett. We will watch here on Sunday 29.08.82.

Hill Sett

Huge sett and difficult to get to. - many holes - 23 in total/10 in use - littered with skeletal remains (skull, femur, scapula and some bristle) - cover is predominantly fir plantation with some ash - evidence of digging persecution in past.

Sett entrance supported by tree roots

Badger country

"The type of country which is hilly, has a sandy soil and contains a high proportion of deciduous woodland interspersed with fertile grassland."

"Sun drenched south facing slope sprinkled with cottages and farms."

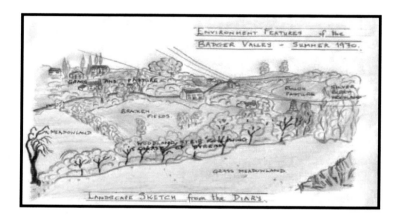

"Cool north facing wilderness fields."
"Rugged limestone ridges."

"A broad valley of predominantly Tintern Sandstone with significant outcrops of Quartz Conglomerate and Brownstones (mainly sandstone) in the valley floor."
"The simple requisites of a quiet life ~ food, water and a comfy bed beneath a safe roof."

Notes of this kind helped us keep a watching brief over the various badger communities in the area and also alerted us to interesting developments which might prove significant or offer some relationship to what we were learning of badger behaviour.

As we hope to show, they have provided fascinating stories and puzzles from many of the major setts as the years went by.

In keeping with our policy of collecting every scrap of detailed information about the badgers, their behaviour and their environment we continued to make use of our daytime visits to the setts to furnish a picture of the world the badgers see and maybe the one they actively choose. The collection of these records drew us willingly into more studies of geology, soil and rocks, landscape, maps and botany as we set out to answer broad questions about their chosen habitat.

At this time we had been fortunate to make the acquaintance of R.D. Hall who had worked with S.R.Ashcroft as students at Marling School, Stroud in the 1960s and had produced results for many of the questions we were interested in.

Their 'Investigation into the Habitat of the Badger in the Stroud Area' gave us details of some of the kinds of information that would be useful and some ideas on how we could use it to formulate a picture of the badgers' world.

What type of location did they choose for their setts? What soil and rock types did they prefer? What slope and orientation of slope did they prefer? What tree canopy, shrub cover and ground cover populated the areas they used?

How far was it to their nearest water supply, to pasture and to their foraging grounds? Their fascinating results showed the following preferences amongst the badgers of the Stroud area in the 1960s.

— *loam soil with small or large stones,*
— *slopes of 20 40 degrees of variable aspect,*
—*deciduous woods or hedgerows with ash, beech or elm tree canopy; elder and bramble shrub canopy, and stinging nettle and dog's mercury in the ground cover - water which was fast flowing, below the setts and within 0-400 yards.*

We used our accumulated information to prepare charts to show details for the badgers of the Lower Wye Valley area. A quick look at the charts plus the Summary of Preferences they reveal finds us studying an all too familiar picture.

The similarities between the results for Stroud and those for the Lower Wye Valley are many and obvious, with a few extra details revealing a liking for or availability of bracken for a comfortable bed and nearby pasture for a ready supply of earthworms.

There is a pattern to what badgers need or prefer in their immediate environment
- the simple requisites of a quiet life
- food, water, and a comfy bed beneath a safe roof, perhaps of branching tree roots or sheltering rocks; and behind that the pulse of life throbs gently as the sun rises and falls and the seasons come and go. The final piece of this serene ideal is to afford them the solitude to enjoy it unimpaired. We hope to encourage people to think like that.

106

The question of how many badgers decide to establish homes in a particular area has been the subject of a great deal of study but Neal and Roper (1991) summarise the findings succinctly saying: Important factors are the diggability of the soil, the hilliness of the terrain and the existence of cover in the form of woodland and hedgerows.

We suggest that in at least some areas badger population density is limited by the availability of sett sites rather than by the availability of food.

Habitat of the Badger in the Lower Wye Valley, Gloucestershire

SETT	ASPECT	SLOPE	SITE	SOIL
Brook	N/NW	31 degrees	Deciduous wood	Sandy loam
Aubreys 1	S	25	Hedgerow	Silt loam
Aubreys 2	S	25	Hedgerow	Sandy loam
Ridge	N/NW	35	Deciduous wood	Sandy loam
New (temp)	N/NW	16	Hedgerow	Unknown
Jims	W	27	Deciduous wood	Sandy loam
Sandy	S	14	Deciduous wood	Silt loam
Sunny	S/SW	23	Hedgerow	Sandy loam
Hill	N	60	Mixed wood	Sandy loam

SETT	Yds. to WATER	Yds. to PASTURE	CANOPY
Brook	0-100 Stream	40	Hazel Willow Holly Birch Hawthorn
Aubreys 1	0-100 Stream	Nil	Hazel Willow Hawthorn Oak
Aubreys 2	0-100 Stream	Nil	Hazel Willow Hawthorn Oak
Ridge	500-600 Stream	Nil	Hazel Ash Hawthorn Elm Beech Elder
New(temp)	100-200 Stream	Nil	Hazel Holly Elder
Jims	200-300 River	Nil	Hazel Holly Beech Elm Birch Ash Hawthorn
Sandy	200-300 Stream	5	Hazel Holly Birch Elm Elder Rowan
Sunny	400-500 Stream	Nil	Holly Oak Hawthorn Sloe
Hill	800 + Stream	300	Ash Spruce

Summary of Preferences

Aspect : Variable   Slope : 0 – 35 degrees

Site : Deciduous wood or hedgerow

Notebook map of Sett Density.

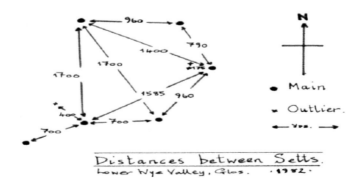

Distances between Setts.

Lower Wye Valley, Glos.   ·1982·

108

SETTLE DOWN
ESTATE AGENTS LOWER WYE VALLEY PROPERTIES

MAIN SETTS , OUTLIERS ,SLEEPING OUT PLACES
AND TERRITORIES FOR THE DISCERNING BADGER .

Extension to a main sett .

. On the crest of a N N/W facing slope .
. 35 degree slope - all soil and debris falls away .
. Sandy loam under limestone strata .
. Deciduous canopy cover .
. Grass pasture adjacent .
. Bracken and grass to gather for beds.
. Water at 500 yds. - slow stream .
Must be seen .

Yes ! This one is nice ....
and it is in a territory where we
are known and accepted as part
of the colony ....so much
less aggro. than trying to
establish ourselves elsewhere !

• House hunting •

109

If it is woodland and hedgerows that are needed, the Lower Wye Valley area offers an abundance of sites many of which have not been adopted and some that have. Neal (1986) reports the findings of the National Badger Survey (1972) that in exceptionally favourable districts for badgers over 100 setts occurred in areas of 10 km2, and that in more typical areas which may be described as good badger country 50 setts per 10 km2 are often found. He also reports some individual areas where much higher sett densities had been found. We decided to map our study area to see where it stood in the hierarchy of favourability for badgers, and to get some idea of how large an area was needed to support a main breeding sett. Using the basis of 10 x 10 km. squares used by the National Badger Survey and multiplying up appropriately it worked out that our area supported a density in the order of 180/200 setts per 10km2.We were delighted to confirm that we were looking at very good badger country indeed.

Taking into consideration our earlier comments about the location of the main setts where changes of geological rock types or formations occur and our observations on the apparent eminent general suitability of the area for badgers it would appear that Neal and Roper's (1991) conclusion that . "In order to survive and reproduce, badgers need a secure, dry sett just as much as they need food explains a great deal about the distribution of setts in any given area."

There appears to be no preference for any particular species of deciduous tree canopy but the low canopy shrubs of hazel, holly and hawthorn are very popular.

This is probably because of the rooting pattern of these shrubs.

Their branching root systems to a depth of 15 - 20 ft. providing a support framework for the sett tunnels. Badgers are known to adopt sites among supporting tree roots.

They are also known to exploit the juncture between solid limestone and underlying softer material. The hard rock forms a strong, impermeable roof which keeps the sett dry and does not fall in whilst the soft stuff makes for easy digging.

The Lower Wye Valley badgers have certainly learnt this trick, and from their home sett they work to exploit and defend a territory of land which provides enough food and food types to sustain them.

One more factor that influences the siting of setts is acknowledged by Ernest Neal and Chris Cheeseman (1996) when they confirm that land which has been previously worked by man is chosen for sett digging. Anything from railway embankments to prehistoric long barrows have been adopted sometimes because they represent the only raised up areas in a flat landscape but also because the soil has been once loosened and is more easily workable no matter how ancient the activity. On some of these manmade mounds trees and shrubs have grown and their roots bind, penetrate and embrace the structures to provide support for tunnels and chambers.

We once visited the setts at Bishopstrow House in Wiltshire to see for ourselves where the first successful filming of wild badgers under artificial light took place, to find that those setts are in prehistoric burial mounds and are of just the type described here.

111

In the Lower Wye Valley the earthwork known as Offa's Dyke is a splendid example of such opportunism.

The eighth century Mercian King Offa had the earthen rampart constructed as a demarcation zone between the English and the Welsh and it is still a significant landscape feature being a raised earth bank into which badgers have dug setts. We got to know of these badgers when a relative discovered them whilst walking her dogs there - actually 'discover' is rather too emotive a word for some of the setts are so active, huge and extensive that thousands of walkers on the Offa's Dyke Waymarked Path must pass them every year and pause to marvel at them.

Because she knew of our interest she passed information about the setts to us and we faithfully recorded it in the diaries and then investigated:

15th. April 1974.
Investigation of sett in Small Hill Wood reported by Susan Hewitt. 14 holes - 3 used for excavation at present – 1. for bedding. West facing at the top of 60 degree slope of Wye valley side in Offa's Dyke.

27th. April 1975.
Investigation of sett in Devil's pulpit region of Offa's Dyke path reported by Susan Hewitt. 13 holes - 7 used for excavation at present. West facing on 25 degree slope and in very stony ground with many collapses. Fresh dung pits in wood bordering pasture.

29th. May 1975.
Susan reported a big sett at Devil's Pulpit Tintern Path.

We took Natasha (Red Setter) to investigate - 17 holes - 7 being used for debris - she says there are even more setts further down the track which we did not get to.

Further information about the environment of each sett was always recorded and is presented in this chart to give a further picture of the badgers of the area.

Reference to the geological maps of the district show that the whole area of this section of Offa's Dyke is exactly where rock types meet.

More precisely, where varieties of limestone (Crease, Whitehead, Lower Dolomite) meet softer, more diggable sandstone (Lower Drybrook Sandstone). So it would appear that the resident badgers have all the features that they prefer in a potential site including some more unusual ones like historically worked soils.

With all this being true our understanding of how badgers choose sites for their setts is tested by the observation that certain of these apparently ideal sites have been developed into vast, ancient setts in continual use whereas other, superficially equally suitable sites, remain as seasonally used outliers often left undisturbed for long periods.

We suppose that we shall never understand the full reasons for this differentiation of development - it is probably something as simple as need for enough living space to accommodate all members of the colony that the territory can support. If we were not so aware of the poor quality of the badger's eyesight we would be tempted to suggest that the Devil's Pulpit badgers may have developed their site because of the view from their 'back yard'- this view.

Tintern Abbey from The Devil's Pulpit Peter Hewitt

Lush meadows of the riverside and the valley floor, rolling forests and wooded streams - rich pickings for badgers and, at one time, for monks.

TINTERN CIRCA 1300?

MAYBE, just MAYBE?

Tintern Circa 1300? Maybe, Just maybe?

The Story of Jim's Sett.

Jim's Sett ~ July 2003

We have already told part of the story of Jim's Sett for it is the one which was so brutally dug and laid to waste in 1970 as described under Persecution. It shines such an inspirational ray of hope that we pick up the story in summer 1982:

Sunday 29th. August

7.05 GMT. We arrived at Jim's Sett in good light. Watching from the woods above the sett was disturbed by horses grazing the edge of the adjacent fields.

7.20 - One adult badger from the recently dug hole below a fallen log - scented the air, detected us and went back inside.

We saw or heard no more as the horses were munching hazel leaves nearby.

Monday 30th. August
Daytime visit to Jim's to find a better watching position.

We chose a bent over tree trunk below the sett where
we could sit held high up.
The wind eddies nastily in this corner of the woods and
successful watching is a case of balancing prevailing wind
direction against the cold air rolling down the slope in the
evening time in deciding where is downwind and where our
scent is being carried.

Tuesday 31st. August
Still evening/no wind.
6.50 GMT. Arrived at new watching seat.
*7.00 - One badger from freshly dug hole on the bank – saw
us and rushed in. Back immediately with another (1
adult, 1 cub). They left for the woods and latrines/two more
followed directly.*

*One from the hole under the fallen log to collect two loads of
loose grass bedding which had been on the mound for some
days, then two from fallen log hole (one adult has a
recognisable pointed tail) to the woods via the play tree.*
*By 7.15 total of eight badgers had left for the surrounding
woods - six adults and two cubs.*

This is the ray of hope, a triumph for the badger colony
once so abused. The sett is back in full use and the badgers
come and go to the accompaniment of the noises of road
traffic/river traffic and distant village and farm life.

December 1982.

The walk from Jim's to the Hill Sett passes a derelict shepherd's hut where a gateway leads onto the Forestry Commission track used for logging and forestry operations. The one post of the gateway is a hollow tree around which is soft mud bearing badger tracks leading off towards the Hill Sett. We were resting near this tree with our two children Ben and Rosie when they noticed that the hollow trunk had a tunnel right through it.

In the hollow centre was a neat, thick and cosy bed of yellow, dry grass perfectly shaped as a nest where an animal had been lying curled up, completely sheltered and dry. We were pleased to find this first evidence of a badgers' sleeping out place in such a charming location.

The walk between the setts is a hard one, steep and rough in places ~ perhaps the badgers had found it so too! We were all resting before the last steep climb and so had they.

It seems the sett was once in deciduous woodland which has been cleared and replaced with a conifer plantation. Characteristically the badgers are reluctant to move far although they have spread into the adjacent deciduous area.

The Hill Sett July 2003 –

Sunny Sett - March 1974 showing a main mound in the hedgerow and, a little further out, the ventilation hole where the dead badger was found.

The Story of Sunny Sett.

Sunny Sett is in a hedgerow at the side of a public footpath and it has, of course, been the subject of daytime visits and occasional observations which tell a tale

....

Thursday 4th. January 1973

The rooting spots and animal tracks that we usually find here have been supplemented by enormous mounds of red, sandy soil spilling from five holes into the lane and the adjoining field. There are fresh dung pits nearby and another latrine 100 yds. away near where 1/2 acre of corn was flattened in mid Summer 1971.

It has been observed, 'they (badgers) are not exactly harmless as they flatten half an acre of corn each year.'

Sunday 17th. March 1974

Sett well used by badgers and rabbits (as usual). Several new holes especially on the field side and a large one in the main hedgerow mound. Recent excavation and a bundle of bedding left out. Strong musky smell from the holes. We found a dead badger strangely located at the bottom of one of the deep circular ventilation holes in the field. We can see his tail and hind bristles but the rest of him is hidden down the tunnel. There are no signs of digging or damage to the entrances, no evidence of gassing or human interference.

Sunday 31st. March 1974

Making our way to the sett the animal paths through the hedges on either side of the lane are obvious as usual and the sett looks undisturbed. The dead badger is still in the deep ventilation hole but the main entrance hole looks well used.

Could this be a natural death in the sett or maybe even a burial chamber? - Observers have reported suspected burials in the sett, and in holes or under burial mounds close to the home sett of a dead badger. One such incident from 1947 is reported by F. Howard Lancum whose correspondent found a dead badger with no visible mark of injury interred in a filled in entrance hole with soil blocking the hole/tunnel to either side of the badger. He observes that 'A man who wished merely to bury out of sight the body of a badger would probably content himself with pushing it well into the hole and shovelling earth over it from the outside, and the fact that the dead badger was covered on the inside of the hole suggests that badgers may have been the sextons.'

He retained an open mind on the mystery as we do with the burial at Sunny sett 1974. The hole was too tight and natural to have been man made and the badger's body was too big to have been thrust in from the outside without leaving tell tale signs. There were better and easier places available for a man to dispose of a body had that been the case. Also the apparent wellbeing of the sett within a fortnight of our discovery tends to rule out any attempts at wholesale destruction by gassing or poisoning.

Intriguingly the diary reminds us that there was a fox skull and top jaw on the debris mound from one of the field holes and an entire fox skeleton - completely white - in the side of the lane leading to the sett.

Bearing in mind the events we have reported from the Brook Sett 1977 (Year of the Foxes) we were left wondering yet again about the relationship between fox and badger in the kingdom of the wild?

The story of this sett and the fragmentary records of its observation provide another ray of hope ....

Sunday 21st. July 1974

Weather - Day - Very hot, sunny, still.

Evening - Warm with breeze. Daytime inspection of Sunny Sett. Sadly the sett has been filled in and flattened by agricultural operations in the field, hedgerow and lane.

Only one hole remains. We fear it is finished.

but then

Thursday 2nd. January 1975

Daytime inspection of Sunny Sett. One sett reopened! Bedding is being taken in from the field. Debris is being pushed out of one entrance onto the field and one into the lane.

and they are still fighting by

29th /30th. December 1982

Daytime inspection of Sunny Sett. Occupied! Fresh dung pits to right of path and fresh soil on the mounds. Some holes have been blocked by plastic sacks but lots of fresh tracks - badger tracks - in the soft mud on the path.

To continue this optimistic train of thought concerning 'rays of hope' for the badger.

The Story of Plantation Sett provides one more example of a good outcome from a challenging situation.

We discovered Plantation Sett in the late 1980s while walking in Forestry Commission woods. We were consciously searching for badger setts in woodland that was new to us by following animal tracks and trails from the roads and rides.

This one is in the heart of a plantation and, interestingly lies where Drybrook Limestone meets Lower Drybrook Sandstone in the surface and underlying rock layers. It was not a fresh discovery as such because on the future occasion of a local badger group alert that there may be badger diggers active in the area we visited Plantation Sett to keep an eye on it to find a group member already on sentry duty.

We cannot decide who was the more relieved when we encountered the sentry and established that neither of us were diggers and we were not going to be involved in a potentially unsavoury encounter. This sett was well known to the badger group!

In the 1990s the plantation was felled and replanted with fir trees - these are after all commercial woodlands worked to produce timber as a crop - but we feared for the prospects for the badgers there no matter what conservation measures were taken to preserve their home.

Current practice requires that a protection zone of a minimum of 20 metres around sett entrances is needed to protect them from forestry operations such as timber harvesting and cultivation - heavy machinery or large falling trees could easily cause subterranean damage and collapse.

Further care must be taken to avoid accidental damage by extraction or cultivation machinery working outside or even across the protection zone. This is in addition to the need for careful timing of operations to avoid the badger breeding season, possibly from December to June but in all events January and February, and to avoid operating at times when badgers may be active between dusk and dawn.

On suitably wind firm sites thought has to be given to alternatives to clear felling of the woodland, at least around main setts, by making the protection zone part of a larger indefinite retention but on isolated, wind exposed sites it may be better to carefully fell the trees in the protection zone rather than leave them to be uprooted by the wind and so cause damage to a sett's earthwork.

Following felling operations no stump removal, mechanical piling or burning must take place within the protection zone.

Drainage, scarifying or ploughing machinery should not enter the protection zone. Tree replanting should be kept at least 3 metres away from holes and should be carried out with hand tools, making as little impact as possible.

The ray of hope we are coming to surrounds evidence that careful treatment of this badger sett and its environment at the time of felling has paid dividends in the future as detailed in these diary entries..........

Tuesday 27th. January 2004.

Daytime visit to Plantation Sett. Main sett is in a grove of elder trees fringed with birch, beech and holly left amongst the fir plantation during the last felling and replanting operations.

The sett area left unplanted measures approx. 12 metres West to East and 20 metres North to South.

At the sett the ground is bare but nearby bracken has been cropped for bedding and moss, brackeny, pine needly, mossy trails lead to sett entrances. The sett area is padded smooth and hard especially around an ancient fallen pine trunk.

Fresh latrines, rooting, and digging from setts. This sett is occupied and active.

Wednesday 7th. April 2004.

Daytime: intermittent clear blue skies and sunshine/showers including some hail. Evening: cool, sunshine and showers.

6.35p.m. GMT. (7.35 BST) Arrived at Plantation Sett. Watching position is in the deep shade of the fir plantation - the forest floor is thick with brown pine needles cushioning footsteps and making for a silent approach.

The sett is bathed in evening sunlight as the deciduous cover of elder, birch and beech has no leaves as yet. Amidst the dark firs the sett is like a stage, brightly lit in a darkened auditorium, awaiting the arrival of the performers. A pair of blackbirds are picking over the fresh soil of the spoil heaps, a distant train rattles along the Severn Valley mainline.

6.57 GMT. The first badger of the evening - a large adult - ambles into view sniffing the air and surveying his kingdom before entering the sett.

7.05. The same badger emerges to wander off westward.

7.10. A smaller badger emerges, crosses the sett and re-enters.

7.15. Small badger is back - much coming and going, by 7.20 these are fleeting grey shapes hurrying to and fro in fading light.

We have a busy sett alive with badger activity, lit in muted shades of green, yellow and white as the dregs of the day's sun funnels through the canopy of branches onto the brown earth floor. The colony has survived and is well.

Nature and commerce thrive cheek by jowl.

On reviewing the diaries we feel gratified that the setts and their colonies of badgers seem to survive all that the world can throw at them.

Sunny Sett was the first we tried to watch huddled against the cold of a frosty winter night and just desperate to see badgers.

That watch was of course unsuccessful - weather, time of year, time of watching - but we have learnt and tried here to convey our knowledge about how badgers live.

Sadly we have also learnt that badgers in various parts of the valley have had to struggle with disease, road casualties, agricultural practice, forestry practice, the neighbours, diggers, baiters, snares and most recently; unbeknown to them as yet; the possible effects of the county minerals plan (quarrying of stone) Is there nothing that these wonderful creatures will not confront and bounce back from? We sincerely hope not.

The stage is sett

Amidst the dark firs the sett is like a stage, brightly lit in
a darkened auditorium, awaiting the arrival of
the performers.

KEEPING IN TOUCH.

The Book Collectors.

We have suggested some insight into the bleak badger watching months of midwinter when an early teatime brings darkness, it is cold, often wet, and the wind blows its warning, or frost dresses the woodland canopy in eerie white and renders the fallen leaves an icy crust underfoot.

Like the badgers we feel tempted to stay at home and sneak out only for essentials - yet there is still a gnawing need to be close to badgers, to share their battle with the elements and know the hardship of their foraging existence.

Common sense mostly prevails and the void has been filled for us, in part at least, by the collection of badger literature that we keep for fireside reading. For sometime E.G. Neal's *New Naturalist Monograph,* Pelican Paperback Edition 1958 to fit neatly in the pocket, was our only badger book and source of reference.

Then in 1974 we were ferreting about in a second hand bookshop in Salisbury, Wiltshire when I came across a thin green book, minus dust jacket and priced at 20p. Howard Lancum's *Badgers' Year,* Crosby and Lockwood, 1954 became the first addition to what has become a treasured library of badger books.

Working from the bibliography of Neal's *The Badger* we soon added Alfred E. Pease - *The Badger - A Monograph,* Lawrence and Bullen, 1898 and began a lifelong read which took twists and turns into many unforeseen avenues of interest.

It was about this time, and in the same bookshop, that we were browsing through P. Jeffrey Mackie - *The Keepers Book* - T.N. Foulis, 1911 Coronation Edition searching for observations on the badger from the game keeping point of view when we made a note for the diary of a tragic tale.
Pages 105/106 Reference by gamekeeper to badgers swimming - subsequent death of badgers after eating poisoned bait laid on an island to destroy carrion crows but it was 2003 before our pocket would stand the purchase of a copy via the Internet simply because it contained that single reference to badgers.

At the time of writing in 2003 the badger shelf now groans with old volumes collected far and wide or new ones eagerly snapped up on publication. They offer an intriguing picture of the changing focus of writing as the pages reveal the early years dominated by the field craft and occupational skills of countrymen who needed to know the animal they were dealing with, for example J.C Tregarthen –

The Life Story of a Badger - Murray 1925, through the application of ecological and scientific method as pioneered by Neal and onto the intensity of surveying and observation applied by Cheeseman and the Ministry of Agriculture, Fisheries and Food in response to the need for more information to help in the evaluation of the badger's suspected role in the epidemiology of tuberculosis in cattle. (Neal E. & Cheeseman C. - *Badgers* - Poyser 1996) or Kruuk in Scotland at The Institute of Terrestrial Ecology (Kruuk H. - *The Social Badger* - Oxford 1989).

Alongside this emerging pattern the collection is peppered with books of raw charm and infatuation ~ *A True Story* by Gordon Burness - *The White Badger* - Harrap, 1970 written with an innocent keenness which reminds us of our own feelings on discovering badgers, Eileen Soper whose watching was so precise that she was able to capture every nuance of posture and movement (Soper E. - *When Badgers Wake* - Routledge and Kegan Paul, 1955 etc.) and the domestic warmth of Sylvia Shepherd in her observations of Brocky at home (Shepherd S. - *Brocky* - Longmans, 1964) and there are those who appear to have almost 'gone native' or should that be 'gone badger', writers like Norah Burke - *King Todd ~ the true story of a Badger* Putnam, 1963 and Chris Ferris - *The Darkness is Light Enough* - Michael Joseph 1986, etc. such has been their commitment to entering the badgers' world on equal terms and become an accepted part of the wildlife community.

The great names of badger writing spread across the map to confirm that affection and concern for the badger is countrywide.

Then there are more names to whom we must apologise for our being unable to assign them to a particular work, area or time frame ~ the likes of Eunice Overend, Beatrice Gillam, Brian Vesey - Fitzgerald, Ruth Murray who stand astride our knowledge as it is written and so passed on.

With the collection of books exclusively or predominantly about badgers nearing completion the search goes on for chapters, paragraphs, tales and reminiscences tucked away in wider ranging books which perhaps, just maybe, tell of the thoughts, opinions or discoveries of these great pervasive influences, and of those of the many knowledgeable authors, enthusiasts and specialists whose work we have yet to discover.

While we are discussing influences, no one who has persevered through the pages of this book will have failed to notice that Dr. Ernest Neal has been probably the greatest influence on our badger study and that of many others recognised here. Nestling deep in a battered folder of press cuttings and badger memorabilia we found this A4 poster for an illustrated talk we were privileged to attend in the early seventies.

Writers of 'Popular' Literature on Badgers –
Where and When.

Writers of Popular Literature on Badgers .
Where and When .

Hans Kruuk 1989
Jim Crumley 1994

Chris Ferris 1995
H. Mortimer Batten 1923

Sylvia Shepherd
1964
Sir A. Pease &
J.Fairfax Blakeborough 1914
A.E.Pease 1896
Paget & Middleton 1974
Peter Hardy 1975

E. Jane Radcliffe 1994
Phil. Drabble 1969 etc.
G.D. Adams 1954   D.J. Watkins-Pitchford 1961
Frances Pitt 1938 etc.   Norah Burke 1964 etc.
Fred Speakman 1968
Michael Clarke 1988
Ernest Neal 1948 etc.   Eileen Soper 1955 etc.
Chris Cheeseman 1996   Gordon Burness 1970
Robert Howard 1981   Monica Edwards 1971 etc.
Pauline Kidner 1993 etc.   Chris Ferris 1986 etc.
Wickham Malins 1974
Howard Lancum 1954   Fred Brown 1990
J.C. Tregarthen 1904 etc.
Richard Meyer 1986

We remember the talk starting with a projected cartoon sketch picture of a badger dressed in academic gown and cap carrying a heavy tome titled 'Homo Sapiens' - the same cartoon or very similar to that which later formed the cover of Dr. Neal's autobiography. –

The Badger Man - Providence Press, 1994.

In the Warminster talk the cartoon was used to set the tone for the evening ~ a man thoroughly absorbed in his subject, an accomplished student who proceeded to entertain and spellbind his packed audience of converts with facts, observations, opinion and anecdotes covering every aspect of badger study. A night for the Badger Diary if ever there was one!

I can barely believe that I once held a signed First Edition copy of the *New Naturalist Monograph - The Badger* - in my hand in George's Bookshop, Bristol, Second Hand Section but this was before the days of avid book collecting and I put it back on the shelf thinking, "We've already got a copy of that." We live in hope of another such chance.

So when the first signs of spring begin to punctuate the countryside again, and the chances of seeing badgers tip to better than evens we do not seem to venture to the fields and woods alone but in the company of shadowy figures secreted against tree trunks or the backdrop of a hedge or thicket, even perched in the lower branches of mature trees and armed with notebooks, binoculars, tape recorders, cameras, red light torches and, nowadays, even silent running video cameras or night viewing and radio tracking equipment.

This is the brotherhood of 'watchers' past and present who have chosen to commit their observations to paper, print and film and remind us that badgers do have lots of friends. Their company is most welcome.

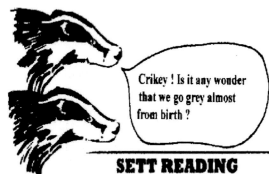

Crikey ! Is it any wonder
that we go grey almost
from birth ?

SETT READING

Essential Studies for Young Badgers

Lumbricus terrestris : *all about earthworms.*

Ancient Earthworks : *a useful guide to sett location .*

Rocks and Soils : geology and sett digging .

Traps and Trapping : *cage , snare , gin and other traps used by men .*

Fox (Vulpes vulpes) : *friend or foe .*

A PLACE IN THE GREENWOOD.

This story begins over a hundred and fifty million years ago when primeval natural forces resulted in the forming of the carboniferous series of sedimentary rocks - limestone, sandstones and conglomerates - in vast layers over the older still brownstones and ancient old red sandstones of the Devonian era, as the geological structure of the Earth's crust was laid down in the areas now known as the Royal Forest of Dean, Severn Valley and Wye Valley.

In the interim between then and now the great rivers Severn and Wye carved great valleys deep through the successive rock layers laid in earlier times, and streams tumbling from the high ground between the rivers eroded their own smaller, shallower valleys which also bit through and exposed the layered structure of the bedrocks.

Now, the southern fringe of the Royal Forest of Dean looms over the River Severn as it hurries along its broad estuarine valley toward the sea at the Bristol Channel, and the steep valley side is deeply incised by numerous valleys and slads each carrying its own bubbling brook into the distant Severn.

So it is that each of these valleys, large and small, expose places where the rock layers from primeval times have been revealed - where hard carboniferous limestone overlays softer sandstones, which in turn overlay dolomitic rocks and limestone shales which rest on Devonian sandstones and brownstones in which the Severn has cut its rich alluvial floodplain and valley.

This Southern fringe of the Royal Forest of Dean, ancient hunting ground for the Kings of England, bears all the hallmarks of its geological history for here the hard horizontal layers of Drybrook limestone have formed tracts of limestone pavement.

It is thinly veiled by the vegetation of the forest floor, which overlie softer Lower Drybrook Sandstone and then give way to various limestones before revealing the brownstones and Old Red Sandstone laid deeper down. And all this laid bare by the erosion of the valleys of rivers and streams.

For fear of frightening off readers who start to believe that this is a book about geology we have consigned the block diagrams which explain and clarify this geological theory to the appendix section at the end of the story.

What is important to our story of badgers in the Forest of Dean is that it is these junctures between rock layers that provide the badger with many of their ideal sett locations

~ a hard, watertight, safe roof over a softer diggable material into which tunnels and chambers can be excavated ~ and this within the solitude of an ancient English forest with lush valley side pastures within foraging range, and often on a gentle slope near running water. It is also true to point out that this coincidence of badgers finding a location for their setts in geological strata is not confined to the Forest fringe - it is a widespread phenomenon and crops up in many surveys and studies concerning the distribution of the badger.

In fact it is so common that a whole new earth science may have been discovered. Geobrockology could be a suitably charming but accurate name for it!

The badger sett we have been watching enjoys many of these features and conditions ~ the solitude of a remote forest, limestone pavement overlying sandstone for the building regulations so to speak, the food fayre of a woodland floor and nearby lush grassland pastures, and the upper reaches of a bubbling brook to quench the thirst but not flood the home.

Because the remote forest is, in modern times, a Forestry Commission plantation we have used the pseudonym 'Plantation Sett' for our 'Place in the Greenwood.'

As we have said earlier we discovered Plantation Sett in the early 1980s when the area was being felled as the timber crop was harvested. The forestry operation revealed a small, self - contained sett which would have been difficult to stumble on when hidden by a full coat of mature trees. However, we were taking the opportunity to walk the newly cleared ground, intentionally looking for badger signs as always, when we noted its location and mounted several fruitless watches in the still of the evenings.

Limestone Pavement thinly veiled by the vegetation of the forest floor. The Sett is in nearby sandstone confirming the site at the juncture between rock layers.

This result was hardly surprising given the scale of the felling operation ~ no matter how careful the operatives were we thought the badgers had probably decamped to more peaceful surroundings whilst the job was done perhaps to return for a future year. We hoped that year may have come when we chose the sett as the subject of a sustained badger watching operation to observe, learn and delight in the community living there.

Our diary of the events at Plantation Sett forms the substance of this story of a summer with the badgers living there.

The present day appearance and probably the very existence of Plantation Sett is due to current practice regulations for forestry operations which were applied during the felling operation of the 1980s.

The fact that these regulations were applied to the operations of the 1980s. has paid dividends for the future wellbeing of the badger sett and its environment Thus by 2004 the sett is detailed in these diary entries

During the bleak winter months when dark evenings and poor visibility make badger watching unrewarding we went about the business of collecting information about the sett and its environment in preparation for watching in the spring. In late January we made a map, took photographs and analysed the soil. The map shows a sett of thirteen holes arranged as eight holes for the main sett, a single hole a little way to the west, and an annexe of three holes to the south east.

Each hole is given an identifying letter and number ~ M indicating a main hole with a debris mound outside and
....
e.g. M1 identifying a specific main hole by number so that it could be referred to in observations and diary notes V indicating a ventilation hole without a debris mound, not large enough for an animal to pass through but sufficient to allow ventilation of underlying tunnels or chambers.

It can be seen that M1 is a large entrance immediately in front of our watching position, M5 is over to our right and the annexe is to our left. Holes M1, M2, M2b, and M4 are arranged around a large branching elder tree around which the ground is padded hard by constant wear from badger feet.

The other significant hard padded area is around the old fallen fir trunk which acts as a play tree. Some of the tunnels and entrances have collapsed leaving most unbadgerlike holes in the roofs of chambers or tunnels, and one sunken area looks suspiciously man made as if a badger dig has taken place there long ago. Although the soil from all the mounds is either sandy loam or clay loam, the proximity of surface limestone pavement to the west confirms the location as the exposed juncture of rock types as explained earlier.

Plantation Sett: Map from the diary.

140

Environment Features.

Aspect	Level ground
Site	Deciduous pocket in conifer plantation
Soil	Sandy loam/clay loam
Metres to water	200 metres to running stream
Metres to pasture	300 metres to valleyside grass pastures
Canopy	Douglas fir plantation, birch, beech, holly, elder
Ground Cover	Sett area: Bracken, moss, pine Needles, Seasonal fungi: sulphur tuft, stinkhorn, Russula species, fly agaric, Chinese hat. Nearby: bracken, grass, bugle, cinquefoil, rosebay, willowherb, wood spurge.

These observations fit neatly with the preferences of badgers choosing their habitat in the Lower Wye Valley detailed in 'The Badger Diaries of Keith and Jane Childs' and included earlier, the only anomalies being that they generally prefer pasture to be closer to hand and to make the sett on sloping ground.

As winter raged by including bitter cold and snow in late February (27th.) which rendered north facing slopes frozen and covered for five nights, and more heavy snow in early/mid march (12th.) which fell gently to dress branches, gates and post tops in six inch fluffy white caps, we acquainted ourselves with the habitat of Plantation Sett whilst eagerly awaiting suitable watching conditions.

That time arrived in early April when we would delay no longer and the 7th. - a cool evening under clear blue skies sporting intermittent showers of rain and hail - found us secreted among the rows of young Douglas firs a cautious fifteen metres to the east of the sett awaiting the emergence of our first badger of the year.

In describing the events of the passing year and the adventures of the badger colony at Plantation Sett we would like to drift a little between science and art, between the concrete and the abstract, between definite observations and emotional feelings.

We would like to convey the whole experience of badger watching ~ the light and colours of the woodland at dusk, the noises and the smells, the unexpected intrusions, the weather, and the company of the host of creatures who are the badgers' regular neighbours.

Wind and sun, cloud and shade, mists, starlit skies and the carpet of the woodland floor; rain soaked foliage glinting in shafts of light which momentarily penetrate once dark corners - all of these things embroider the minutes and hours of waiting alone with your thoughts.

There are many things in the natural world which, although anticipated and almost guaranteed, always create a feeling of magic ~ finding warm, rich brown eggs in the nesting box of the chicken house is one, and the clutch of new potatoes beneath the haulm unearthed by the garden fork is another.

You know they are there, you have planned for them to be there but every time the thrill of discovery is the same. Badger watching is like that too, every time, but especially on the first watch of the year.

The atmosphere of expectation is positively primiparous as you stare unblinking, silent, unmoving, waiting for the first black and white face hovering in the sett entrance to test the air.

So it was on....

Thursday 22nd. April. Where we pick up the story of Plantation Sett.

Tonight we waited only fifteen minutes before the first badger emerged from M1 Directly in front of us, in bright sharp light.

April evenings see the light mellow from bright to diffuse yellow before darkness creeps in from the edges to frame a fading green picture and the grey shapes scurrying about the sett have been indistinct but tonight they are out early.

*Between 8.05 and 8.40 we enjoyed watching a pair
drag three loads of bedding into M3 from beyond the fallen fir
trunk.*

*Having completed this housework they could be seen
play fighting until darkness fell and we crept away with the
strong smell of musk wafting to us on the breeze.*

Thursday 29th. April.
*We waited for an hour beneath overcast showery grey
skies with a bright moon masked by drifting storm clouds.
Owls hoot, peacocks whistle and the 7.37 wails its hooter
on the Severn valley mainline.*

*A grey squirrel climbs zig - zagging up the dry brown
under branches of the fir plantation, oblivious of us; then there
is musk scent on the air again before the pair emerge to
groom themselves and each other near M2. They are joined
by three more from M2 - two adults and a smaller badger, not
a 2004 cub maybe a yearling still living at home?*
*The group spends time stretching up the elder trunks
which dominate centre stage, scratching and nibbling at the
mossy bark. Five badgers tonight - a pair and a threesome at
ease but soon off to forage.*

This group of three became a regular feature of our
watching, sometimes just the three, sometimes in company
with others, but they were recognisable and helped us work
out the membership of the colony.

On *Saturday May 1st. the wood is blanketed by light mist hovering between the trees and we wonder if our scent will be held down by the blanket of mist and we will be detected but a gentle breeze cools our faces to confirm we are downwind of whatever air movement there is and we can settle to enjoy cuckoo, peacock and female tawny owl punctuating the dusk birdsong with their strident calls.*

Emerging at 8.06 there is much urgent coming and going by the adult badgers in a manner which past experience suggests they may be caring for cubs below ground and are reluctant to leave them for long. Surely they should at least be keen to come out by this time of year but there is no sound at all. We remark that these are remarkably quiet badgers.

By May 5th. The light filtering through the canopy is rendered pastel green by the fresh young leaf growth and the fresh rain on green leaves at eye level makes them look white especially when stirred by the wind and peeped at through the bare branches and broken twigs of the fir plantation.

There could be badgers everywhere. - Woodpeckers tapping over in the oaks and beeches herald the emergence of the pair and then shortly the group of three from M2. They groom and play fight as a group with the pair being particularly playful. They are all yickering, yelping, rolling, chasing and biting playfully - so much for the quietness of only four days ago! The pair return below ground and the group of three melt away into the woods west.

We are getting to know these badgers, five again tonight, and to formulate a picture of the resident population but needless to say the picture was going to develop and clarify as the year wore on.

Our watch on Thursday 6th. May is summarised in the diary as 'wonderful watching tonight'. Three of us were settled by 7.30 and enjoyed the dusk birdsong until 8.04 when the first badger appeared to make his routine tour of the sett and its environs before an adult and cub emerged together from M4 - our first cub of the year.

Others joined them from M2 and M4 including the group of three ~ play fighting, wrestling a brief mounting are interspersed by coming and going when we can hear them yickering when they are out of sight in the woods nearby. Then two cubs, one much larger than the other emerge from M2, we witness a little more housework from the adults as one bundle of dead leaf bedding is dragged backwards into M1. At 8.30 the group of three departs for the woods and the cubs retire below ground. MS is being used to our far right but we cannot see it properly from where we are and we creep away in fading light.

Badgers entering and leaving the sett, and making excursions to the woods and latrines, make a headcount difficult but we thought the group of three plus a pair with two 2004 cubs were at home tonight. The size difference between the two cubs was to influence and guide our understanding of the colony later in the year. Observation 'markers' like this are very important in knowing who is at home!

Compare this with a week later....

Wednesday 12th. May.
Again settled by 7.30, camera ready, good light conditions, muggy but no rain.

We waited until the light faded at 8.50 - saw nothing, heard nothing, smelt nothing!

There are many possible reasons why badger watching is beset by these blank nights. We would like to explain some of them here because they colour the experiences of so many patient watchers.

1 Someone or something has been near the sett in the daytime. The paths are used by walkers, dogs, deer, forestry workers, etc.

2 What tiny air movement there is carrying our scent over the sett and alerting the badgers to our presence.

3 The evenings are getting lighter and therefore the badgers are coming out later, but we did wait until dark.

4 They were already out as we arrived and were either frightened in or they had already left for a night's foraging. This is not the pattern so far this year.

5 They fed well the previous night after torrential rainfall and slept in.

6 The badgers have left the sett or moved temporarily to join other badgers for the summer community living although it is very early for this. Whatever the reason blank nights cause significant worry until badgers are seen again confirming that they have not been harmed.

Friday 14th. May.

After a sunny, warm day the wood pigeons are cooing, the crows are kaaaing and the tawny owls are kee-wicking before the first silent grey shape sneaks away to the woods and a second hurries nervously from M2 to M4. The group of three are playing, wrestling and chasing as always and can soon be heard yickering away in the woods leaving the air heavy with musk scent, while the pair are nervously sniffing the air at M2 but did not emerge until we left in fading light.

We think that something has alarmed the badgers and that the pair are still protective of their cubs keeping them below ground until safety is assured. More promise of good watching still to come this year. The remainder of May allowed us to see evenings of badgers playing, rolling, grooming and chasing in 'follow my leader' fashion with long lines of badgers loping nose to tail into the woods and back home again.

The splayed elders are used for scratching and nibbling as badgers reach as high as they can on tip toes (about four feet) before they lose their footing and tumble back onto the mound.

They also run and jump onto sloping branches where they bear hug or balance on the trunks as they nibble and lick the moss.

The housework continues with the digging out of fresh soil from M5 producing tennis ball size lumps of heavy clay as evidence of their tough, sticky work.

During these evenings we are amused by a pair of blackbirds making daring low level manoeuvres across the open ground of the sett, occasionally landing to pick through the leaf litter and fresh excavations. A shrew darts and stops, darts and stops between the firs, peacocks in the slad compete with the constant hiss of road noise in the distance.

By mid June the woodlands appear to be suffering from drought and Met Office records confirm that May has been very dry with only 45 percent of average rainfall more than half of which fell in only two days. Mean temperatures have also been above average across the whole of the U.K. The lower branches of the Douglas Fir plantation seem to have drooped presenting more of a screen to watching, brushing our heads and shoulders. Although these branches seem dry and dead they are too pliable to snap easily and have drooped with the rest of the plant in need of water. By late June the splaying trunks of the big elders over the main sett have been neatly stripped to a line as high as a badger can reach on tip toes. Moss, of course, is damp in dry conditions and harbours slugs. This represents a source of moisture in desperately dry times and these badgers have taken all they can possibly reach.

By Tuesday 1st. June there is some change in the social grouping of the badgers at Plantation Sett.

**Entrance M2.The dark rows of the pine
plantation can be seen behind.**

**Entrance M1 Directly in front of our watching
position.**

**Entrance M5. The tunnel has collapsed
leaving a deep entrance gully**

**Peeping at the sett through the bare branches
and broken twigs of the fir plantation.**

Counting Badgers.

Right, this is what we'll do!
He's definitely seen three of us come out together!
You, Titch, sneak back in and come out of another hole:
and you, Paleface, make a big show of leaving for the
woods and then creep back behind the bushes and show
yourself at the other side of the sett. I'll create a distraction
by rolling and scratching here.
He won't have a clue how many of us there are!

The group of three has become four as the bigger cub from the other family has joined them. They are behaving as two pairs grooming and playing, musk scenting and stretching into the elders, before leaving as a group. Later, at 8.45 the other pair and their small cub are nervously bobbing in and out of M2. It would seem that this small cub is going to stay with its parents whilst its bigger sibling joins the other family. Is this what happened last year resulting in the familiar group of three (two adults and one yearling cub)? More group dynamics shortly because more changes are imminent.

Saturday 5th. June

7.50: First badger from M3 to inspect the area, soon followed by a second, quick visit to the latrines north of the sett and then to play near M3.

They move near to M4 where others come out to join them for 40 minutes of play, wrestling, yickering, mutual and individual grooming and scratching in a big group of seven. The air is heavy with musk scent.

8.30: They all move off to the woods north and west before returning to M5 for some serious housework - five loads of soil are dragged out during this watch alone. Eventually a family of three returns to M4 while the group of four can be heard north of M5 and are returning there intermittently to work.

Although the two groups are identifiable and separate they are beginning to associate more and behave as one big group or colony as in the play session of 5th.

This example of animals from different parts (holes) of the same isolated sett gradually integrating as parents and cubs grow more confident is one aspect of the development of community living during summer months when large numbers of badgers are seen together at the same sett.

This year the numbers seen together at one time has increased as the groups have integrated.

In Scotland where, in the Highlands at least, the setts are more widely scattered Mike Tomkies (Out of the Wild - Jonathan Cape 1985) gives an example where he found evidence that in Autumn one badger family would take its cubs, born between early February to mid April, to visit another family over a mile away.

It was as if the parents were introducing the youngsters to each other in a 'match making' exercise, giving them a chance to get to know each other before possible pairing later.

He has other interesting observations on the dispersal of family groups which are relevant to things at Plantation Sett 'junior setts' and the annexe; 'yearling cubs still at home' and the small adult.

Of course circumstances dictate behaviour; a heavily populated sett may remain independent of others for social interaction but an isolated family has to move their cubs to meet others, or receive visitors from away.

We are interested to follow the Plantation population to see if other badgers arrive during the late summer and autumn, or if the Plantation families move away to find other groups to mix with. We secretly hope not, the watching here is too good to be spoilt.

This may be a suitable point at which to look at a chart of all the watches at Plantation Sett 2004 to illustrate how the social interaction of the community changed as the summer wore on.

Summary of Watches - Plantation Sett 2004.

Date .	First Emergence BST.	Badgers seen .	Total.
7 April	7.35	1 large ,1 small , plus singles .	?
15 April	8.30	2 large , 1 smaller .	3
22 April	7.45	2 pairs.	4
29 April	8.30	Pair plus pair and yearling .	5
1 May	8.06	Pair plus pair and yearling .	5
5 May	8.35	Pair plus pair and yearling .	5
6 May	8.04	Pair plus yearling / pair plus two cubs .	7
12 May	-	None	0
14 May	8.15	Pair plus pair and yearling .	5
20 May	8.14	Single plus group of four .	5
26 May	8.18	Single / pair plus yearling .	4
1 June	8.16	Two pairs plus pair and cub .	7
5 June	7.50	Pair plus cub / group of four .	7
9 June	8.30	Pair .	2
14 June	7.40	Pair / Single / Group of four .	7
25 June	7.53	Seven plus four maybe .	7/11?
6 July	7.57	Group of three .	3
9 July	7.40	Six / single / single .	8
15 July	8.07	Three / three / single / single .	8
21 July	8.02	Three / two / single cub / single .	7
28 July	8.16	Three / single .	4
2 August	8.00	Several .	?
10 August	7.55	Single / three / single .	5
22 August	7.40	Group of three .	3
24 August	8.10	Group of three / pair / single .	6
31 August	7.32	Group of three / single / single .	5
2 September	7.35	Single / single / group of four / single .	7
27 Sept .	-	None .	0

The end of June - Friday 25th. finds the woodland freshly washed and damp from two days of heavy showers and several torrential downpours.

The track to the plantation is head high with bracken and Rosebay Willowherb and the brown needleless lower branches of the Douglas Firs have lifted, they are not dead but respond to a good watering like green plants.

We are watching in company with the blackbirds and crows and by 8.00 there are seven badgers all from M3, who are in no hurry to leave the sett area as we are treated to a full hour of group playing and grooming activities and more housework - this time four loads of leaf litter bedding dragged into M1 or M3 from west of the sett.

Again a headcount is difficult because of all the coming and going but the most counted together at one time is seven. As the big group begins to disperse west there is still activity in and out of M1 close in front of us.

Two look like this year's cubs one comes toward us but a click of my tongue sends him back.

There may be another family of two adults and two 2004 cubs using M1 tonight but that would make a great number for a small sett. However such numbers have been recorded before and all the main holes were used tonight.

Badgers seem like neighbouring people in this respect. Sometimes you spend time with them and go to their houses and gardens and at other times you would rather be alone or with your own family. On the way home we disturb a young fox cleaning himself on the forest track. The dregs of the evening sun show off his dusky colours, almost black on his back and tawny brown to greyish underneath. But he wants to be alone and melts away silently into the beechwood when he hears us approach.

Balls of sticky clay from the excavation of M5.

The splaying elder trunks neatly stripped as high as a badger can reach on tip toe.

From the diary December 2004. Illustration of the group of three becoming a group of four (Tuesday 1st. June), the possibility that the small cub will stay home as a yearling, and of the arrival of visitors for the summer 'community living.'

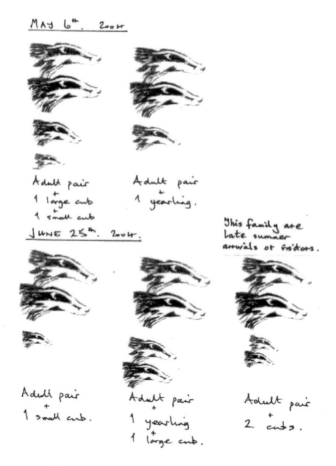

MAY 6th. 2004

Adult pair
+
1 large cub
+
1 small cub

Adult pair
+
1 yearling.

This family are late summer arrivals or visitors.

JUNE 25th. 2004.

Adult pair
+
1 small cub.

Adult pair
+
1 yearling
+
1 large cub.

Adult pair
+
2 cubs.

Badger population at Plantation Sett 2004.
Changes in social composition and interaction.

It was in June that the track to the badgers' wood was changed causing us great concern. Our walk to the Plantation had meant leaving the stone surfaced Forestry Commission logging track to proceed downhill on a narrow footpath before bearing left and continuing to where the sett could be reached by turning between the rows of firs.

The fir trees are in rows with six feet between trees, the rows being about that same distance apart, the effect being to create straight, narrow avenues between the rows. By the 14th. the downhill stretch of footpath had been cleared all the way down to our left turn and by the 20th. had been further opened up by a mechanical digger and bulldozer. The footpath has become a levelled roadway some 8/9 feet wide.

We feared that the disturbance suffered by the badgers in the early eighties was about to be repeated just as we had 'adopted' the sett for a years watching. It appeared that the track was being prepared for forestry operations. On the 21st. we contacted the Forestry Commission to find out what was to happen. They said that they knew nothing about the new roadway but, as it was on their land they should, and would investigate.

We arranged a site meeting for that very afternoon. By the time we met forester Stuart Hunt on site he had done some 'homework' and discovered that an agricultural building project on the higher slopes of the Severn valley had been granted temporary permission to gain access to their site for heavy goods by opening up the track to create a useable roadway. The permission had been granted two years earlier, before his appointment, and had been forgotten but it was all recorded for him to find out.

The access permission was apparently necessary because the narrow, twisting lanes up from the Severn valley had made delivery of heavy goods impossible, but temporary access from the B4228 via the new roadway solved the problem.

All was well. The track clearance was not going any closer to the badgers. Stuart looked at the plantation and its badger sett with us and confirmed that he anticipated any further operations to be at least five years off judging by the size of the trees.

He also confirmed the features of past forestry management around the sett and agreed to check that it was recorded on forestry operations maps so that it would be properly treated when further operations became necessary. We felt quietly pleased that a valuable badger protection issue had been raised and received sympathetically.

This explains why, in the still peace of a warm, humid August evening the first badger had just emerged at 8.00 when the reversing alarm of a lorry reasonably near by struck a discordant note. We do know who was more alarmed - the badger or us - it was us because the badger trotted straight into the woods north whilst we feared the worst. Deliveries at this odd hour would likely interfere with watching. However our walk home revealed that pallets of FARMSCAPE 'Anthracite' corrugated roofing sheets had been delivered to the top of the temporary access road and they duly disappeared, presumably down to the building site, in the next few days and we were never bothered by further deliveries coinciding with our watches.

This incident with the lorry reversing alarm was one of several disturbances, some perfectly natural, some man made that coloured our watching during July and August.

Our cartoon 'The Remote Woodland Location' is a pastiche of some of the intrusions suffered in the tranquillity of Plantation Sett.

Hence, following a very hot afternoon on Tuesday 6th. July we were sitting in the cool of the evening, in position by 7.10, and during our half hour wait for badgers a train sounds its horn on the Severn valley mainline, a single engine, propeller driven aircraft drones immediately overhead.

There are distant gunshots and an emergency vehicle sounds its siren all along the B4228. Why do we bother to approach quietly?

Well apparently these things may be disturbances to us but seem to be a fact of life for the badgers who can distinguish unerringly between imminent danger and distant activity and life goes on ....

Tuesday 6th. July.

7.57 - 8.10: The badgers are nervous - startling each other and wary of our presence near M1 No playing or wrestling - a little communal grooming and then an intense spell of bedding gathering. One female gathers several loads of green bracken from east of the sett and delivers it deliberately to M2, bypassing M3 on the way. She collects balls of dropped bedding from her trail and delivers that to. Another collects from woods west and several times carries scraps in her mouth back to M2 and M1. A busy night continues as we sneak away at 9.10 while they are away collecting again.

Thursday 15th. July.

There is no birdsong! There is rustling and crackling of twigs in the woods behind us as three fallow deer are approaching following the path we have just trodden. They see us and rush off.

Cause for concern

The footpath to the plantation as it had been and the new roadway following widening by mechanical digger.

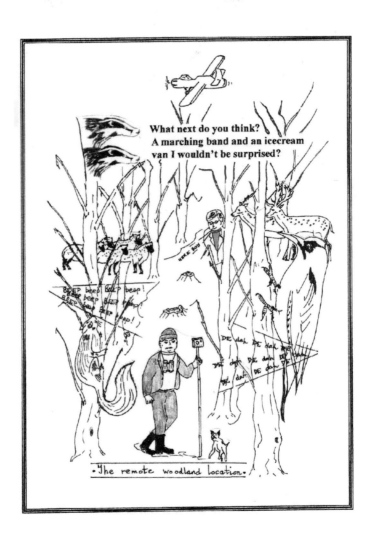

8.17. First badger tonight heralds a big night of 'climbing' and scrambling into the elders. One falls off a low sloping branch which he has just mounted with a run and a leap. Trying to hang on, he swings down to gain a landfall on tiptoes.

Engrossed in this we are taken by surprise when there is a hissing noise behind us and a small badger runs past us ignoring available holes to follow earlier badgers into the woods. This has been quite a 'they're behind you' night for badgers and deer.

8.50. We left thinking that frequently we could hear yickering noises of badgers out of sight. There again may be more badgers here than we counted on sight.

Wednesday 21st. July.

Again there is no birdsong except the occasional plaintive peep, peep, peep and other alarm calls. Birds are, however, still dipping down to pick up tasty morsels from the sett mounds.

8.02. First badger from M5 straight to the woods north returning in just five minutes - maybe an urgent call of nature.

Suddenly three dogs - black collie cross, brown woolly Alsatian type, brown terrier mongrel, race onto the sett area. Shocked we watch them zig zag over the whole area noses intently down, and then away between the firs as quickly as they arrived.

Looking back to M5 a bemused badger on full alert is also watching the dogs but only runs below ground when a man in a red jumper appears to call the dogs. We instinctively wish we could run and hide too!

This is probably a first hand experience of one of the possible explanations for the blank watch of 12 May offered earlier - someone or something has been near the sett in the daytime.

164

After an evening's fitful watching we leave at 8.50 trying desperately not to crack any twigs underfoot or rustle branches overhead. On turning for one last look at the sett in its stagelit spot amongst the firs a badger is watching us from M1- a small 2004 cub - which emerges to trot up over the mound by the elder clump. This cub lives in M1 with its mother.

A question lurks in our minds. What has happened to the birdsong? This is one of the subliminal benefits of having an excuse to sit alone with your thoughts in the solitude of the woodland at dusk.

You notice things like the quite sudden change from vibrant trilled choruses to plaintive peepings and it draws you on to find out why.

Reading revealed that, very basically, birdsong is inextricably associated with the season in which it is delivered and that although some birds may sing at any time of the year, they are most vociferous in spring when establishing a territory.

As summer approaches and paired birds turn their attention to nest building, laying eggs, incubating and raising their young, the songs of many species become more intermittent or subdued, or even cease altogether. We were relieved to learn that this is probably what was happening to the dusk birdsong in the plantation. And what of those peep, peep, peepings and alarm calls?

Well we also learnt that there is a distinction between song and calls - another fascinating diversion for another day.

So July passed with these and other watches, faithfully recorded in the original diaries, allowing us to enjoy the badgers engaged in the full range of activities embraced by a colony at peace in their remote corner of the greenwood.

At the beginning of August we decided to move our watching station forward two trees (about twelve feet) which places us about 18 - 20 feet from M1. This will give us a better view of the play area by the fallen fir but restricts our already patchy view of the mounds at M5. Thankfully our silhouette is still broken by the firs and their broken lower branches.

As well as the better view of the play area we also hope to get a more complete view of the whole sett. If we could see the whole sett area from a single watching station we would know exactly how many badgers live here by now, but we cannot always be sure if those that leave for the woods and latrines return or not because all of their holes and paths cannot be seen from a single vantage point. This makes a precise population count impossible. More watching time and better recognition of individuals is part of the answer so observations go on.

Monday 2nd. August.
7.30. No birdsong except the occasional plaintive cheep, cheep and single high pitched whistles (tree creeper?) but these are calls not songs?! The air is hanging, humid and warm beneath the canopy and the smell of stinkhorn fungi (Phallus impudicus) is overpowering.
The 'powerfully foetid stench' (Oxford Book of Flowerless Plants - Brightman and Nicholson - 1966) from the six that have burst through the pine needle litter of the woodland floor will surely mask any human scent tonight even though we are much nearer.

If we get detected tonight I have a serious body odour problem that no one has been tactful enough to tell me about! At the edge of the M1 mound the thick white stems are sporting their olive green jelly caps alive with visiting insects.

Between 8.00 and 8.55 several badgers emerge to go straight to the woods north east. None cross the sett nor is their any work, play or noise. Perhaps they can't stand the smell either. By 9.00 all is quiet. On the walk home we take huge lungful of crisp, clear night air to help flush out the smell of fungi endured for 1 1/2 hours - the badgers are probably doing the same somewhere not far away.

Thank goodness that by Tuesday 10th. August the stinkhorn have wilted and the smell is gone.

Stinkhorn fungi: glowing white in the half light under the canopy.

An ideal evening - countryside watered gently by light rain over several days - faintest breeze from the west - allows us to witness a big scratching session (delirious is the word which comes to mind) for the group of three before they split up and one tries to move off through the firs east. This takes him downwind of us; he smells us and races back to M5 sounding the alarm with a gruff bark and guttural purring, like purring with your teeth chattering. We leave them nervously dodging in and out in the gathering gloom.

167

This is the wettest August on record, many areas having received double the average rainfall - 154.2 mm. in the South West and South Wales being 168 percent of the average. This must be providing excellent feeding on earthworms brought to the surface by the rain - very good for fattening up badgers for the winter - and means that badgers need to be on their feeding grounds rather than loitering by their setts in idle pursuits like playing chase. As August turns to September, Summer to Autumn, the amount of time spent near the sett after emerging gradually reduces. The diary reveals telltale notes such as:

Sunday 22nd. August: Need a torch with a red light for future watches. This after trying to see previously crisp black and white faces made distinctly brown by the muddy underground conditions of the damp season.

Tuesday 24th. August: Tonight, very brief stay at sett, little play, yickering off west, used red torch on last badger as he moved away at 8.20.

To see badgers for any length of time now you must really know your badgers and, more important, all of their territory. To know where the sett is, is not enough. You must know their trails and feeding grounds to hope to see them at length and even then it is chancy.

We still watch until darkness falls enjoying the elder berry feast of the wood pigeons and blackbirds, the thrushes picking over the bits that drop down from the treetop meal, but time spent with the badgers is short. We laugh at mud stained badgers and their naughty appearance, and treasure the occasional evening spent at home in play, grooming and particularly scratching:

Thursday 2nd. September.

By 8.00 there are four scratching and playing, yickering and chasing through the trees. One adult - a boar - does not take part in play but sits scratching and scratching and scratching.

The youngsters come back to tempt him, nipping his toes and running away, but he does not want to know and by eightish they all leave for the woods. As we leave at 8.15 there is still one at home at M3 popping up to test the air but it is too dark to wait on any longer. The watching season is all but over.

But the business of watching out for badgers goes on with our regular daytime visits to the plantation which throw up interesting insights into the day to day work of the badgers and their encounters with both wild and domesticated neighbours. On one such walk we came upon a whole flock of sheep on the temporary roadway near to the badgers. For any sheep buffs reading, they were Clun Forest breed: 'hardy, prolific and adaptable; a long body with a small head held erect giving an alert appearance; the lambs mature early and they produce a fleece of 6-7 lbs.' (Book of the British Countryside 1973) and they had turned the ground into a mess of hoof prints and droppings.

Nearby preparations were being made for the Lydney Sheep Fair and Sales to take place the following day and we wondered if some of the livestock had made a run for it a day early.

The agricultural qualities of the breed would be well known to all attending to do business at the sales. The sheep had only just scattered as we approached when two fallow deer crossed in front of us. Without careful use of wildlife tracking skills it would be possible to assume that a huge herd of deer had passed this way had we not seen the sheep and then the deer for ourselves.

At the sett we notice which holes are being used for fresh excavation, and the identification of the holes is refined.

By mid September the holes in the M3 region have been named and numbered as M3, M3b, M3c, etc. as they are all significant holes but close together ~ it has not always been possible to see which one, exactly, the badgers use as they come and go in that area. When presented as a chart of digging activity during the autumn and winter months useful clues are provided about where the best watching may be had in the spring and summer.

Combining this information with what we have seen of bedding being taken in to prepare chambers for sleeping we have a picture of an active and thriving sett featuring freshly dug chambers furnished with bracken, leaf litter, moss and pine needles populated by badgers who have played, groomed and cohabited in groups and pairs. The expectation for watching in spring 2005 is enormous, the waiting almost unbearable.

Saturday 6th. November.

October has been a very wet month compared to the average. The digging from M1, M2 and M4 is wet and sandy bearing deep claw marks and footprints.

That from M3c beside the fallen fir trunk is drier - rich sandy red soil - and there is a trail of leaf litter, moss and bracken into the hole. Small bundles and scraps have been left along the trail. This M3c hole will be very interesting next springtime 2005. Digging of new, or perhaps enlarging of chambers, and lining with fresh bedding suggests that a nursery is being prepared?!

Holes Used for Fresh Digging: Autumn/Winter 2004.

Date	Holes Used for Fresh Digging				
03 Aug.	M1	M2	M3	M4	M5
11 Sept.	M1	M2	M3c	M4	M5
27 Sept.	M1		M3c	M4	M5
07 Oct.	M1	M2		M4	
06 Nov.	M1	M2	M3c	M4	
10 Dec.	M1	M2	M3	M4	M5
19 Dec.	M1	M2	M3	M4	
31 Dec.	M2				

Entrance M3c

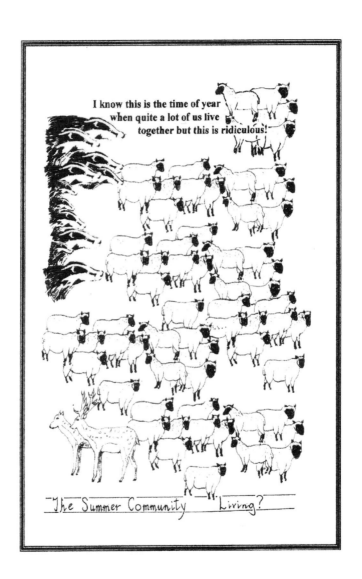

BLOCK DIAGRAMS TO SHOW EXPOSURE OF
JUNCTURES BETWEEN ROCK LAYERS BY EROSION

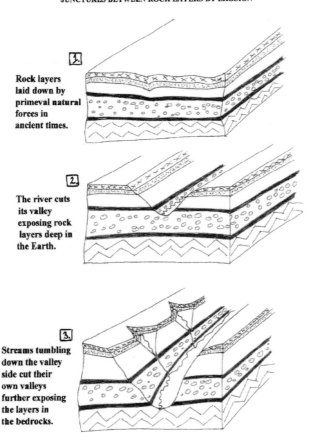

1. Rock layers
laid down by
primeval natural
forces in
ancient times.

2. The river cuts
its valley
exposing rock
layers deep in
the Earth.

3. Streams tumbling
down the valley
side cut their
own valleys
further exposing
the layers in
the bedrocks.

PAWPRINTS ACROSS OUR HISTORY.

There is a lot of evidence that badgers are following in the footsteps of men and in turn, leaving their own paw prints on the history of the landscape. Wherever men have dug the soil to create their homes, fortifications, monuments, fields, workplaces, transport systems; in fact anywhere that soil and rock has been hewn and scattered, badgers have followed to capitalise on the better digging conditions created in terrain once worked by man.

On Salisbury Plain in Central Southern England 4000 years ago men of the Bronze Age and Neolithic periods were busy building burial mounds to cover and mark the resting places of their dead. Huge amounts of soil were excavated from the hard chalk landscape and piled up to make the barrows and mounds, long and round ones that dot the Plain. Badgers searching for places to dig their setts and establish their homes have found that these ancient mounds suit their needs admirably on several counts.

The soil is much easier to dig than virgin chalk downland and after several thousand years of settlement is compacted enough to allow effective tunneling.

In a predominantly flat area the sides of the mounds provide a slope into which the tunnels can be driven and down which excavated material can tumble away; and furthermore some of the barrows contain stone structures which improvise as a ready made roof over a safe, warm bed - all that the burrowing badger requires. In the course of their burrowing the badgers dig through anything which lies in their path and scuff out the broken soil and artefacts to make room for their tunnels and chambers.

This is causing a problem. Apparently vital evidence about our past has been disturbed, broken up and scattered across the surface terrain so defying any study of the sequential nature of man's development.

The 1999 NT Archaeological Site Monitoring Report revealed that 35 percent of archaeological sites on the Stonehenge Estate have been damaged by burrowing animals, both badgers and rabbits. In real terms this means that on Salisbury Plain there are badger setts in 'more than 52 Bronze Age barrows or Iron Age enclosures'.

This 35 percent should be viewed in relation to the other findings of the report - 30 percent of the sites have been damaged by Human Impact (6 percent levelled by ploughing/26 percent by footpaths and building works), 13 percent damaged by livestock and a further 22 percent damaged by vegetation because 'root systems severely damage the underlying archaeological layers'. (Trench One - Channel 4 Television Issue 10 March 2001).

No figure was given for the damage done by military training exercises since the late 19th. century, although Phil. Harding (Trench One) does point out that the area has been largely unploughed since Roman times and because it was used mainly for sheep grazing it remained in its unchanged state prior to the Army acquiring it in the early 19th. Century.

It would appear that there are lessons to be learnt here - for the best part of 2000 years the area benefited from grazing by appropriate livestock (sheep) and a lack of ploughing reduced the risk of sub surface damage. Some measures have been taken to limit the damage from military training exercises but no one is going to pretend that 'No Digging' signs are adequate protection against tank manoeuvres and live ammunition are they?

However, badgers, probably one of the few ever present influences on the landscape of Salisbury Plain at least since prehistoric times, seem to be shouldering the blame for many other injustices in the management of the countryside and our heritage. The point I am coming to is that badgers have discovered and established a habitat in the prehistoric earthworks of Salisbury Plain - one of many examples of them exploiting the activities of men to their advantage.

The Barrow sett at Bishopstrowe House hidden amongst the rosebay willow herb and the giant beeches.

Bishopstrowe House in Warminster, Wiltshire is now a sumptuous country house hotel with manicured grounds sweeping down to a crystal clear chalk stream, and slightly more demanding walking to a naturalised area featuring a wooded ancient burial barrow.

In 2002 we were fortunate to make the acquaintance, in a round about fashion involving the family network, of the Head Gardener who arranged for us to visit to see the place where the first film of badgers under artificial lighting was made by Ernest Neal and Humphrey Hewer in the 1950s.

At that time the house was a private family home, the location having been chosen via their family network alerting them to the presence of badgers in their wood.

It was a great privilege to walk to the ancient long barrow first investigated by Ernest Neal before he settled on another area nearby in the house grounds for the successful experiment with habituating badgers to artificial light strong enough to allow movie filming under electric light bulbs.

That badgers occasionally using a prehistoric long barrow sett should become the stars of such a momentous filming occasion has taken on new meaning in light of the recent discussions about Salisbury Plain. In the reception of Bishopstrowe House we were shown a flashlight photograph of badgers leaving the barrow sett at dusk taken by a visiting celebrity. They must have been direct descendants of the film star badgers of the fifties - stars photographing stars as it were.

**The wooded prehistoric long barrow
at Bishopstrowe House.**

At Saltdean near Brighton a long running badger problem (March 1988 to November 2003 at least) was eventually explained by referring to historic land use by man. The problem centred on a large main sett in the grounds of four houses which had caused significant problems for some considerable time.

Over 40 sett entrances with their associated tunnels and chambers had resulted in many tons of soil being excavated. Paths, patios and other garden features had been undermined rendering up to 80 percent of some of the garden areas unusable and a danger to elderly residents, visitors and children. Droppings were being deposited near to one of the houses presenting a potential health hazard.

After measures ranging from an attempt to exclude badgers from the sett to humane dispatch of some of the animals had been tried Professor Stephen Harris was commissioned by The National Federation of Badger Groups to investigate the case when more than 500 protestors prevented D.E.F.R.A. from culling further badgers under licence.

As part of the investigation a survey of archaeological records showed the sett to be constructed in a lynchet - a ridge of soil formed by prehistoric farmers who were ploughing the hillside above where the houses now stand. The overspill of soil provided the badgers with easy ground for digging when a development of flats destroyed their ancestral sett. This explained why the badgers were so determined to remain on their chosen patch - other locations in the district were not suitable because the soil had not been 'prepared' as the lynchet had been some thousands of years ago. The badgers are now being offered alternative accommodation in artificial setts near to their problem home and in a suitable habitat where they will be welcome if they can be persuaded to stay. Prehistoric earthworks certainly meet with the approval of twentieth century badgers.

Move forward a little in time and we find King Offa busy directing the construction of his now famous Offa's Dyke along the borderlands between England and Wales in 780 AD.

The dyke consists of a high bank or wall with a ditch in front that is to the west of it, and may have been intended to keep the Welsh out of his Saxon kingdom. Although some alternative thought suggests that it may have served as a highway rather than a barrier.

The wall of the dyke is constructed of whatever the material may be through which it runs, earth or stone, thrown up out of the ditch. J.H.Hewlett, in his early book 'Offa's Dyke', draws attention to the destructive effect of the plough in flattening out stretches of the earthwork, the development and eroding quality of a footpath as a right of way, deliberate levelling for agricultural and territorial purposes, and the slow destruction by trees, vegetation and rabbits.

'For miles and miles the great wall is so honeycombed with warrens that the whole vast fabric of it is as rotten as wood eaten through and through by beetles'. This is all remarkably similar to the situation on Salisbury Plain and we can confirm that badgers have not missed this opportunity to use ground once worked by man.

On one Gloucestershire stretch of the dyke you can join the long distance footpath at a stile and way marking fingerpost. Follow the path for just 250 paces north and you come to huge ancient setts which spill their sandy red soil down the steep slope of the bank and into the ditch.

Further along there is an often active three hole outlier sett spilling onto the path, and 500 pace further again an enormous main sett of at least 52 main entrances plus ventilation holes and tunnel collapses, the mounds spilling west and east from the bank of the dyke. All this is within a single stretch of about a mile and then there are other setts within easy walking distance either way, some of them permanently occupied main setts and other seasonal outliers.

J.H. Hewlett may well have been describing the work of badgers.

These ancestral setts are busy with fresh digging, rooting spots and fresh latrines under a rich canopy of ash, oak, holly and fir. They have precipitous wooded slopes or the rugged valleys of seasonal streams to scramble down to the riverside fields of the Wye, or the pools and succulent grass pastures of the Tidenham Chase lands, one time hunting ground of Kings, within their range.

They have vantage points on limestone crags towering over the Wye gorge from which to scream their defiance to the Welsh.

Battle of Edge Hill 1642. A significant building on the battlefield at Radway village was the King's Leys Barn from which the King's sons were reported to have watched until the position became threatened by the action as the Royalist forces forsook their vantage point on the steep down of Edge Hill to march down the valley and engage the Parliamentarian army. This information was gleaned from the TV programme 'Two Men in a Trench' screened on March 11th. 2004.

The programme found the remains of the building in the middle of a ploughed field, only a pile of rubble having been left undisturbed by the plough to mark the site of the Civil War barn. A local badger expert identified an outlier badger sett in the pile and, due to the protected status of the badger and its sett, the excavations to reveal the foundations of the barn were restricted to the edge of the mound leaving the sett undisturbed.

Badgers had selected the previously worked ground once again, or perhaps they had been there since the floor of the barn had afforded them a safe roof over a dry home - it would not be the first time that badgers had exploited this potential in a building.

In 2004 the snowdrops were blooming early at Kingston Lacy House, Wimborne, Dorset and the garden opening for the Snowdrop Walk was brought forward to Sunday 1st. February.

**Badger setts on Offa's Dyke
spilling onto the long distance path.**

The Japanese and Tea Gardens are located within an area of mature woodland and are styled as a natural garden. They were planned and established in the early 1900s. to provide a walk between the Kingston Lacy house and the kitchen garden.

Estate records show that they were planted with snowdrops and daffodils as well as trees and shrubs to provide colour and shade throughout the year. Ideal for badgers.

The secluded Tea Garden with its levelled area for a thatched tea house, traditional ornaments and planted areas is backed by steep banks cut during the hard landscaping of the original garden.

On the banks freshly denuded of vegetation by the work of the restoration project there is evidence that badgers have established setts, spilling white limestone soil from the fresh digging with other older holes and collapsed tunnels nearby not so freshly white.

The Forest of Dean Badger Patrol newsletter of Spring 1987 reports that badgers were digging their setts in the steep sides of flood banks and drainage channels on the flat Severnside Plain giving rise to fears of potential flood risks and of dangerous drainage blockages. The Dean Group began working with the Gloucestershire Trust for Nature Conservation, the Severn Trent Water Authority and the Ministry of Agriculture to discuss and implement ways of dealing with the problem.

By the autumn the Severn Trent Water Authority were still concerned that the setts in the flood banks may cause a breach. A site meeting revealed that the water authority had already commenced a programme of measures to dissuade the badgers from using the flood banks at both of the problem locations.

Electric fences and one way gates had been tried but evidence suggested that they had not been successful. The Dean Group agreed to survey the area and make recommendations, work which resulted in the problem at the one site being solved by the water authority carrying out a small amount of work on the flood bank. The survey also confirmed that the second site was more difficult to resolve. The water authority applied for a licence to translocate the badgers but the Dean Group were not happy that this would be a satisfactory solution in the long term.

The translocation of badgers is known to be problematic - it involves risk of interfering with the social organisation and territorial boundaries of badger colonies and the determination of badgers to return to their original chosen location is quite legendary. Further survey work and observations attempted to ascertain the likely numbers of badgers in occupation.

The Dean Group's recommendations suggested that work should be done on the flood bank to ensure that the badgers could not tunnel through the bank thereby weakening the defences.

Discussions and a second site meeting resulted in the water authority withdrawing the application to translocate. The programme of dissuasion would continue and the Dean Group would monitor the situation in the meantime.

The long list of incidences where badgers have taken advantage of civil engineering earthworks as diverse as the embankments of roads, railways and canals, mines, coal tips and rubbish dumps, under buildings and major roads, and also in flood defence and drainage schemes is the twentieth century continuation of a story which has left its footprints and paw prints across thousands of years of, quite literally, the history of our land.

MEALS - on - WHEELS

THE RAIDER IN THE CHICKEN COOP.

It is high summer in Bishop's Tawton. A balmy mid summer night on the coast of North Devon when the air is still warm, hot even, long after dusk and the upstairs windows have been left ajar perchance the sea breeze will cool the house. Overlooking the steeply sloping garden and neighbouring fields the windows look down on a post and wire enclosure set aside for chickens. Tonight as on many such nights the door to the run has been left open affording the chickens' free range over the garden and into the adjoining grassland. There has been no trouble with foxes for many years and the nightly ritual of shutting in the hens has been neglected or rather has faded to a distant memory. The chicken house, a traditional wooden coop, stands in the enclosure and is home to black rock and warren laying hens which furnish the kitchen and table with a daily supply of warm fresh eggs.

184

At 3.00 am. there is a commotion in the chicken house, clearly heard because of the open windows, then a spell of quiet followed by another commotion.

Something is distressing the hens but the man of the house is away on business and the shadows of the garden path are forbidding.

More commotion, and so the lady and her children, armed with a torch and broom and fiercely attired in pyjamas and dressing gowns begin their adventure to investigate. Being careful to clatter the broom handle on the path and fence to announce their arrival and scare off any intruders the enclosure is approached. The searching beam of torchlight picks out feathers everywhere on the ground, and some still floating down to settle in the dust. Peeping out of the coop the black and white face of a badger betrays the culprit which makes its escape at surprising speed through the open gate and across the field.

Morning and daylight reveal that the lighter, more agile warrens have escaped injury by roosting in the lower branches of overhanging trees but two of the heavier black rocks have been lost.

A visit to the neighbours to explain the disruption at dead of night reveals that they too have seen a badger in the chicken run but this was on the night following his raid and this time the coop was firmly closed and the badger was seen perched astride the roof hoping to find a way in or perhaps just patiently waiting for the door to open. Badgers are opportunist feeders taking whatever appetising fayre comes their way.

DID SOMEONE
SAY A MYSTERY
NEEDS LOOKING
INTO?

THE PARK ESTATE MYSTERY.

In summer of 2004 I was shown a sett in the grounds of Lydney Park Estate high on the crest of the Severn valley side where the Old Red Sandstone of the valley side gives way to limestone and coal measures near the Forest of Dean rim. Within the space of a few paces the soil in the badger mounds changes from rich red sandstone to browny/black coal (lignite) ~ another example of badgers establishing their setts at the juncture of rock types.

The Forest of Dean region is like a large basin made of layers of Devonian and Carboniferous limestones in which the coal seams are located, but as the description implies the layers are not flat, they are folded into a basin shape which is high on the edges and sunken down in the centre. This whole basin structure is held high above the valleys of the Severn and Wye rivers on vast layers of Old Red Sandstone and, even older, Brownstones. The journey from the River Severn at Lydney to the heart of the Forest of Dean basin means travelling up the steep side of the valley passing over fields of rich red soils, and then over the raised rim of the basin.

It is here that the coal bearing rocks are present nearest to the surface - exposed by countless millennia of erosion.

Notebook Sketch of the Park Mystery Landscape.

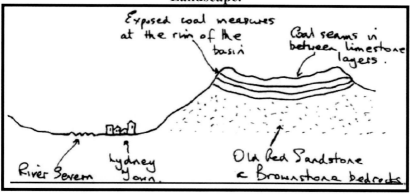

Trenchard is the first coal bearing seam encountered on the journey up the Severn valley side and over the rim into the Forest of Dean plateau. Exactly at this point badgers have chosen to settle and excavate setts. This is why the soil from some holes at the Park Sett is rich red and sandy but very nearby it is dark and coaly. It is a large sett, one of many I suspect, of several holes and although there is no fresh excavation there are recent latrines nearby This is a bluebell wood beneath primarily sycamore interspersed with ash and birch, it is remote, enjoys stunning views and is disturbed only by the gentle hum of the agricultural economy all around in thousands of acres of forestry plantations, grazing pastures and arable fields.

Now you may well be thinking that this is just one more example of Geobrockology at work and there is nothing unusual about being shown a picturesque sett in idyllic surroundings - it happens all the time once family and friends know of your interest.

The story of the Park Sett is of further interest because of the tragic mystery which unfolded there in late spring 2005.

My daughter 'phoned early to say she had been walking with her dog Brodie at the Park Sett where they had found a dead badger cub outside one of the holes.

The Park Sett in bluebell season with the dead cub.
Saturday 14th may 2005.

Sunday 15th.
I visited the sett to inspect the find. It was a small cub lying loosely curled up at the foot of one of the mounds. It had no visible sign of injury and was not noticeably thin or emaciated. It had a full healthy coat.

188

Also it lay there undisturbed until July 6th. by which time it was a skeleton disintegrating into the leaf mould with just a few scraps of fur and bristle still evident. Nothing and nobody had moved it or pulled it about by feeding off it or attacking it.

The exposed skull revealed no intersagittal crest confirming an age of less than one year.

The lower jaw was broken in two at the chin and is detached from the skull where it is usually strongly jointed at the angle of the jaw. Rosie also revisited and said that she suspected broken ribs.

These are all the signs of a badger knocked in a car accident when the animal turns to face the assailing car at the last moment before impact so suffering facial injury. However there was no outward sign of this.

The first suspicion is a road accident but the cub died in mid May probably not long after first being allowed above ground and the nearest road is 250 yards away. This seems a long journey for such a youngster, and a long way to limp back severely injured to die close to home.

Starvation is a possibility but again this was not evident although it doesn't take long at that tender age.

If the mother had been killed on the road and so failed to return home that could account for the cub being outside looking out for her, but what of the broken jaw?

Could that have happened since and are the jaw bones that rigidly set in one so young anyway? The cranial plates making up the skull were still loosely jointed; perhaps the jaw is like that also. If the condition of the jaw was an injury then suckling would certainly have become painful, impossible even.

Coincidentally in the May week that the cub was discovered Pauline Kidner and The Secret World Wildlife Sanctuary staff in Somerset issued a television appeal to dog walkers to be particularly vigilant as badger cubs had been dragged from setts by dogs going below ground.

189

Maybe this had happened at the Park but it would seem likely that the cub would bear the signs of an attack vicious enough to kill it?

Illness or disease is a further possibility - I wonder if the cub had died where it lay or if it had become ill and died below ground to be scuffed out by other badgers keeping the sett clean?

I suppose something as innocent as an accident in rough play, and badger cub play does get very boisterous, could have been responsible for this tragedy.

There were no signs of human activity - no digging, no disturbed soil so I am inclined to discount that distasteful option on this occasion. Then there is the relationship between badgers, foxes, and other wildlife. That has resulted in fatalities before, as has parental rejection.

The possibilities are manifold and I suppose we shall never know the facts of The Park Sett Mystery but it is interesting to review the total of what we know of badgers from a lifetime of casual study and so try to piece together the evidence into a reasonable explanation. Maybe, just maybe, we will stumble on something else which we should do to prevent such a thing happening again.

191

NEWS FROM WILTSHIRE.

In 1966 Beatrice Gillam published the results of her survey of the distribution of badger setts in Wiltshire in the Natural History Report of the Archaeological and Natural History Society. There was a considerable amount of 'Geobrockology' implied in her conclusion that the Greensand hosts clearly the higher proportion of setts, and in particular the wooded Upper Greensand slopes where the digging is easy.

The preference for wooded slopes probably satisfies the need for adequate cover and seclusion as well as the structural support afforded by tree roots securing the roofs of setts in sandstone soils of a light and friable nature.

We have taken the opportunity to visit setts in the Upper Greensand in the region of the upper reaches of the River Wylye, an area where Upper Greensand lies over Gault Clay, where streams can be dammed before reaching the Wylye to form artificial lakes like the ones at Stourhead and Shearwater.

The setts we visited are located where the side of a valley of Greensand pastureland used for sheep grazing gives way to woodland plantations.

It features indigenous oak, ash, beech and birch along the fringe of a mature Norway spruce conifer plantation.

The plantation clothes a ridge and knoll of higher ground between valleys and sees setts on aspects facing S/E and North. They tend to occupy approximately 45 degree slopes in the woodland fringing the pasture. The shrub canopy is predominantly holly and blackthorn, the ground cover is bramble, bracken, foxglove and broom. The area showed fresh digging from the holes, large patches of the woodland floor churned up by badgers foraging for food and latrines full of glistening black dung. We still can't explain why we were shocked to find that the sandy soil spilling from the gaping sett entrances really is green!

This combination of ecological and geological features offers the Greensand badgers a wonderfully diverse environment digable soils clothed in trees and shrubs for sett building on gentle slopes, a secluded coniferous forest and rich grass valleys, and freshwater streams and ponds all within reasonable foraging distance.

The day provided us with some of our best ever badger sett location photographs showing the 'ideal' mix of pasture, woodland, seclusion and slope.

Note book Sketch of the Greensand Region.

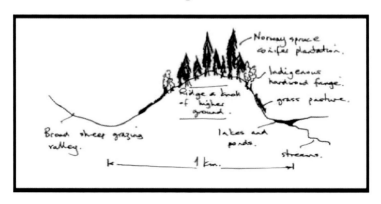

And the sand really is green

Within this range the badgers also have the gardens and patios of sympathetic householders who realised that badgers were visiting their gardens and ponds when the motion activated security lights were triggered by them.

Now the animals have become accustomed to the lights and can be watched as they come to enjoy the nightly supply of food put out for them. The reports of the badgers' visits and the questions thrown up by their numbers, sizes and behaviour helped us piece together a probable picture of their activities as the year progressed.

March 18th. 2005.

The fayre tonight is peanuts and raisins, cornflakes and homemade scones. As described the security lights were activated at 8.10 by the single male who arrived to feed for 25/30 minutes. Apparently he returned at 3.00 am. but we, of course, were long gone by then! There have been two badgers coming but now its only one. Why is that?

Probably the smaller female has given birth to cubs in the sett 150 metres away uphill in the woodland fringe overlooking the pasture, gardens, ponds and streams in the valley below.

April 9th.
The female visited the patio feeding station for the first time since Monday 14th. March - 25 days in total.
She came with her much larger mate for peanuts, raisins and cornflakes.
Could it be that she has ventured away from the sett where her cubs have been born, for the first time? News of cubs coming to feed is eagerly awaited.

April 30th.
For the first time three badgers visit the patio for food ~ not a cub but a third adult.

May 31st. Tuesday.
The badger pair have brought a cub with them tonight. They do not like the honey sandwiches which they leave for the foxes to clear up, but all three tuck into the peanuts.

Their visits are from 10 o'clock to 10.50 and then again at 3.20 am. Also 'the big badger is sitting on the smaller one. I'm a bit worried about it' the report reads.

We confirm that this is part of the bonding process of the badger family marking each other with musk scent from their anal glands which they rub on each other to mark them as part of their social group. This need to mark existing and new members of the community would fit exactly with the needs of a growing family moving further away from home in search of food. As I was responding to this question I was reading Badgers in Our Village by Fred Brown and he uses the same words to describe the musking process as one badger apparently sitting on another. His observations are excellent and heart-warming.

June 21st. Summer Solstice.

Five at the patio this evening - two big ones and three smaller ones ~ the whole family are coming together as they would to such a regular supply of food. By July 3rd. this is a regular occurrence.

July 10th.

It very often happens that one badger arrives earlier than the others to take food. Why is that?

We suggest that this is probably the boar on his early tour of the sett and environs before returning to call out the others. As the boar is probably living separately from his family - in the same sett but using different chambers - it has commonly been observed that he will make this kind of 'tour of inspection'. This boar has included the patio on his route to take full advantage of his authority.

July 12th.

The badgers are fighting over the food. Is that normal?

There has been a prolonged spell of hot dry weather. The ground everywhere is bone hard and the earthworms are staying deep down therefore none of their favourite and main food source is available temporarily. This squabbling is a sign of hungry badgers desperate for food. Weather records for central southern England confirm that Spring 2005 (March - May) saw only 79% of normal rainfall and Summer (June - August) saw 90%. Although this does not sound extreme local conditions were very dry.

July 17th.

Six badgers feeding tonight. The windows are open on these summer nights and the report asks about the smell of musk scent on the air which has not been noticed so strongly before.

Our suggestion is that this large gathering and the strong musk scent indicates that the whole social group is living and operating as one big group. Large numbers of badgers seen together is a common sight at this particular time of year.
It is thought that this kind of activity allows for the members of the group to familiarise and, all importantly, become marked with scent to identify them as acceptable members of their community. At any other time of the year it is unlikely that such large groups will be seen together.

July 25th.

Six again, between 9 o'clock and 9.20. I am visiting and enjoy the chance to see two fully grown adults, two 2005 cubs and probably (judging from their size) two 2004 cubs all arriving for peanuts, dog food and the special treat which I took along - Crunchy Nut Cornflakes drizzled with honey from a squeezy bottle.

Tonight they savoured every morsel even licking the patio stones where the honey was drizzled shortly before.

The matter of how much and how often and at what times of the year should the badgers be fed came up in conversation. Should they be able to find enough at this time of year without extra feeding?

We all talk again about the squabbling probably caused by shortage of earthworms, this at a time of year when wild food might reasonably expect to be plentiful.

We discuss the semi hibernation torpor which sees badgers spend much time asleep in winter, leaving their setts infrequently and taking little food. They rely on fat reserves put on during the plenty of summer - back to the impact of summer drought and its longer term effect on badger welfare and chances of surviving the winter. Inadequate fat reserves because of summer shortage of food and water reduces the chances of surviving the winter torpor fit and well to feed up again in the spring.

We decide that regular feeding of sensible amounts throughout the year is the best measure. The food should be not so much that the badgers become dependent on it and manage without foraging for their own wild food but should represent a welcome supplement, a treat which can be relied upon. After all, what would happen to dependent badgers if you were unable to provide anymore for whatever reason? They must be able to return to surviving without what you provide. In the meantime the treats you furnish might just see them over periods of shortage.

Badgers are, of course, genuinely omnivorous and you will soon find out what they really like but peanuts, raisins, cornflakes and honey and those homemade scones did the trick in Wiltshire.

Pair on April 9th

July 14th.

Here they come

Full House for supper

Farewell

Bibliography.

Keith and Jane Childs are keen collectors of books on badgers and their writing has been influenced by reading widely on the subject. However the intention has been to offer something fresh and original in the observations reported and this list covers publications which are specifically mentioned or which have particular bearing on this work.

(Automobile Association 1973) Book of the British Countryside. Drive Publications

Adams G.D. (1954) The Hill of Light. Constable, London.

Barron R.S. (1976) The Geology of Wiltshire .A Field Guide. Moonraker Press.

Bennett D.P. & Humphries D.A. (1965) Introduction to Field Biology. Edward Arnold, London.

Bradbury K. (1974) The Badger's Diet in Paget R.J. and Middleton A.L.V. Badgers of Yorkshire and Humberside. Ebor, York.

Brown F. (1990) Badgers in Our Village. Grafton Books.

Burke N. (1963) King Todd - the true story of a badger. Putnam, London.

Burness G. (1970) The White Badger. Harrap, London.

Burton M. (1950) Animals and their Behaviour. Edward Arnold, London.

Burrows R. (1968) Wild Fox. David and Charles, Newton Abbot.

Childs K.G & J.L. (2004) The Badger Diaries of Keith and Jane Childs. Private

Clark M. (1988) Badgers. Whittet Books, London.

Cresswell P., Harris S. & Jeffries D.J. (1990) The history, distribution, status and habitat requirements of the badger in Britain. Nature Conservancy Council.

Crumley J. (1994) Badgers on the Highland Edge. Jonathan Cape, London.

Drabble P. (1969) Badgers at My Window. Pelham, London.
Dreghorn W. (1968) Geology Explained in the Forest of Dean and the Wye Valley. David and Charles, Newton Abbot.

Edwards M. (1971) The Valley and the Farm. Michael Joseph, London.

Ferris C. (1986) The Darkness is Light Enough. Michael Joseph, London.
Ferris C. (1995) Beneath the Dark Hill. Swan Hill, Shrewsbury.
Forest of Dean Badger Patrol. (1987) Spring Newsletter. Autumn Newsletter. F.of D. Badger Patrol
Forestry Commission (1995) Forest Operations and Badger Setts. Forestry Practice Guide 9. Forestry Practice Division.

Gardiner C. (1975) Four Men in Horror Attack on Badger. Western Daily Press and Times and Mirror.
Gillam B. (1966) The Distribution of Badger Setts in Wiltshire. in The Natural History Report of the Wiltshire Archaeological and Natural History Society.

Hall R.D. & Ashcroft S.R. Investigation into the Habitat of the Badger in the Stroud Area. Marling School, Stroud. Unpublished.
Hardy P. (1975) A Lifetime of Badgers. David and Charles, Newton Abbot.
Harding P. (2001) The Pain of the Plain in Trench One, Issue 10 March. Channel 4 Television.
Harris S. & Skinner P. (2002) The Badger Sett at Lustrell's Crescent/Winton Avenue, Saltdean, Sussex. National Federation of Badger Groups.
Hewlett J.H. (1921?) Offa's Dyke. Simpkin, Marshall, Hamilton & Kent. London.

H.M.S.O. (1973) Badgers Act 1973. H.M.S.O. London.
Howard R. (1981) Badgers Without Bias. Abson Books, Bristol.

Institute of Geological Sciences (1981) Geological Maps
of England and Wales Solid and Drift Edition Chepstow Sheet
250 Monmouth Sheet 233. Ordnance Survey.

Kidner P. (1993) Life with Bluebell. Robinson Publishing.
Kingston Lacy House. The Restoration of the Japanese
Gardens in Lady Walk. Site Information Boards. The
National Trust. Kruuk H. (1989) The Social badger. Oxford
University Press.

Lancum F.H. (1954) Badgers' Year . Crosby and Lockwood,
London.

Mackie P.J. (1911)   The Keepers' Book. T.N. Foulis,
Edinburgh.
Malins W. (1974)   Bully and the Badger. Robert Yeatman,
London.
M.A.F.F. (1976~1997) Bovine Tuberculosis in Badgers.
M.A.F.F. London.
M.A.F.F. (2000)   TB and Cattle Husbandry. Report of
the independent Husbandry Panel - The role of cattle
husbandry in the development of a sustainable policy to
control M. bovis infection in cattle (Dr. C.J.C. Foster, C.
Morris, Dr. P.Teverson, Dr. R. Phillips) M.A.F.F.London.
M.A.F.F. (2001) TB and Cattle Husbandry -
Government response to the report of the Independent
Husbandry Panel. M.A.F.F. London. Mortimer Batten H. (1920)
Habits and Characters of British Wild Animals (1928 Ed.)
Chambers, London.
(1923) The Badger Afield and Underground. Witherby,
London.

National Trust (1999) NT Archaeological Site
Monitoring Report - Stonehenge Estate. NationalTrust.

Neal E.G. (1977)   Badgers. Blandford Press, Poole.
Neal E.G. (1986)   The Natural History of Badgers.
Croom Helm, London.
Neal E.G. (1994)   The Badger Man - Memoirs of a Biologist.
Providence Press, Ely.
Neal E.G. (1948)   The Badger. Collins, London.
Neal E.G. & Cheeseman C. (1996) Badgers. T. & A.D.Poyser,
London.
Neal E.G. & Roper T.J. (1991) The Environmental
Impact of Badgers (Meles meles) and their Setts in
Meadows P.S. & Meadows A. (1991) The Environmental
Impact of Burrowing Animals and Animal Burrows.
Oxford University Press.
Met. Office (2004) http://www.met office.gov.uk/climate/uk
& (2005) 2004/index.html UK Climate & Weather Statistics.
Met. Office.
Nicholson B.E. (1966) The Oxford Book of Flowerless
Plants. Oxford Uni. Press.

Paget R.J. & Middleton A.L. V. (1974) Badgers of
Yorkshire and Humberside. Ebor, York.
Pease A.E. (1898) The Badger. Lawrence & Bullen,
Covent Garden.
Pease Sir A. E. & Fairfax - Blakeborough J. (1914) The Life
and Habits of the Badger. The Foxhound.
Pitt F. (?) British Animal Life. Westminster Press, London.

Ratcliffe E.J. (1974)   Through the Badger Gate. Bell,
London.
Readers' Digest (1969) AA Book of British Birds. Drive
Publications.

Shepherd S. (1964)   Brocky. Longmans, London.
Soper E. (1955)   When Badgers Wake. Routledge & Kegan
Paul, London.
Speakman F. (1965) A Forest at Night. Bell, London.
Stephen D. (1963)Watching Wildlife. Collins, London.

Simms E. (1958) The Language of Badgers in Voices of the Wild. Country Book Club.

Television Programme (2004) Two Men in a Trench .Ch.4TV.

Tregarthen J. C. (1904) Wild Life at the Land's End. John Murray, London.

Tregarthen J. C. (1925) The Life Story of a Badger. John Murray, London.

Tomkies M. (1985) Out of the Wild. Jonathan Cape .

van Lawick -Goodall H. & J. (1970) Innocent Killers. Collins, London.

Watkins - Pitchford D.J. (1961) The Badgers of Bearshanks. Ernest Benn, London.

Weekly Argus (1979) Badger Kill Brings £150 Fines Total 15/02/79.

Williams S. (1972)   Must the Badger Die? Daily Mirror . 07/08/72.